MAGNIFICENT RECOLLECTIONS

By

Cecelia Frances Page

iUniverse, Inc.
New York   Bloomington

MAGNIFICENT RECOLLECTIONS

iUniverse books may be ordered through booksellers or by contacting:

iUniverse
1663 Liberty Drive
Bloomington, IN 47403
www.iuniverse.com
1-800-Authors (1-800-288-4677)

Because of the dynamic nature of the Internet, any Web addresses or links contained in this book may have changed since publication and may no longer be valid. The views expressed in this work are solely those of the author and do not necessarily reflect the views of the publisher, and the publisher hereby disclaims any responsibility for them.

ISBN: 978-1-4502-2711-7 (pbk)
ISBN: 978-1-4502-2712-4 (ebook)

Printed in the United States of America

iUniverse rev. date: 6/22/10

Contents

Preface

MAGNIFICENT RECOLLECTIONS is a marvelous book of 70 short stories and articles. There are a wide variety of topics such as adventure, science, health, history, landscape, fantasy, education, travel, human interests, religion, archaeology, philosophy and other topics. SCIENCE TOPICS are What Do Animals Know?, Earthquake Tragedy In Haiti, Meteors and Meteorites, Weather Conditions In The World, Alternative Energy, Laws Of Nature, India's Great Scientist And Inventor—Jagadis Chandra Bose, George Washington Carver's Accomplishments, Swans Are Graceful, Present Day Dinosaurs, Anastasia's Garden Techniques and Magnificent Rainbows. HEALTH TOPICS are Pyramid Power, A Healthier Way to Eat, Old Fashion Cooking, Hemp—The World's Miracle Crop and Anastasia's Garden Techniques. HISTORY TOPICS are Gobekli Tepe—The World's Oldest Temple, Life In The 19th Century, Shambhala and Underground Egyptian Temple Discovered In The Grand Canyon.

More subjects are LANDSCAPE TOPICS including Dubai, A Modern Country In The Middle East, California—Land Of Resources, Country Life, Knowledge About Antarctica, South America, Land Of Opportunity and Phenomenal Discoveries About Lake Vostok. ADVENTURE TOPICS are Beyond The Horizon, Wild Sailboard Adventures and An Interplanetary Adventure. FANTASY TOPICS are Tasper the Ghost, Revisit Alice In

Wonderland, Imaginary Figures and Tale Of Bliss. <u>EDUCATIONAL</u> <u>TOPICS</u> are Reading Enrichment, Experiences In Classrooms and Become Well Educated.

<u>HUMAN INTEREST TOPICS</u> are The Tea Party, Louisa May Alcott—A Well Known American Writer, The Tea Party, Best Friends, About Famous Film Stars, How Television Effects Our Lives, Identical Twins, The Shopkeeper, Brad's Conflicts, Experiences At A Pub, Important Moments, Giants In The Soloman Islands, Boriska—Indigo Boy From Mars and Elderly Years. <u>RELIGIOUS</u> <u>TOPICS</u> are Invisible Reality, The Last Supper, What Is Missing In The Bible?, Churchgoers, Inner Dimensional Contacts, An Experience In Cosmic Consciousness and The Last Prophecy Of Peter Deunov. <u>PHILOSOPHICAL TOPICS</u> are Why We Need To Know God and What You Need To Know About Yourselves. <u>OTHER TOPICS</u> are Speculations And Answers, Continue Being Creative, Cabin Homes On A Cruise Ship, Hatchback Five-Door Electric Ford, Music In Daily Living, The China Set, About Banks And Bankers, A New World Economy and The Mystery About Crop Circles.

About the Author

Cecelia Frances Page has been writing since she was 19. She has written 50 books. Cecelia has published five, original screenplays and three, original poetry books which are entitled <u>Cosmic Dimensions</u>, <u>Vivid Impressions</u> and <u>Significant Introspections</u>. Cecelia Frances Page has written over 500 original poems. Several of her poems are published in the World's Best Poems Of 2004 and 2005. The original screenplays are entitled <u>Walking in the Light</u>, <u>Flashbacks</u>, <u>Celestial Connections I and II</u> and <u>Adventures In Lemuria I and II</u>.

Cecelia Frances Page has had 42 books published by iUniverse Incorporated which are entitled Opportune Times, Imagine If…, Fortunately, Mystical Realities, <u>Westward Pursuit</u>, <u>Power of Creative and Worthwhile Living</u>, <u>Magnificent Celestial Journeys</u>, <u>Extraordinary Encounters</u>, <u>Brilliant Candor</u>, <u>Expand Your Awareness</u>, <u>Seek Enlightenment Within</u>, <u>Vivid Memories Of Halcyon</u>, <u>Awaken To Spiritual Realization</u>, <u>Celestial Connections</u>, <u>Phenomenal Experiences</u>, <u>Celestial Beings From Outer Space</u>, <u>Awesome Episodes</u>, <u>Horizons Beyond</u>, <u>Incredible Times</u>, <u>Fascinating Topics</u>, <u>New Perspectives</u>, <u>Certain People Make A Difference</u>, <u>Very Worthwhile Endeavors and Circumstances</u>, <u>Magnificent Celestial Journeys</u>, <u>Interpretations Of Life</u>, <u>Tangible Realities</u>, <u>Amazing Stories And Articles</u>, <u>Extraterrestrial Civilizations On Earth</u>, <u>Adventurous Experiences</u>, <u>Relevant Interests</u>, <u>Impressionable Occurrences</u>, <u>Significant Moments</u>, <u>Remarkable World Travels</u>,

Infinite Opportunities, Random Selections, Stimulating Awareness About Life, Marvelous Reflections, Magnificent Recollections and The Future Age Beyond The New Age Movement and more.

Cecelia Frances Page has a B.A. and M.A. in Education with a focus in English, Speech, Drama and Psychology. Cecelia is an excellent pianist. She is a piano and voice teacher, vocal soloist, author, educator, drama director, philosopher, photographer and artist. Cecelia believes that creative abilities and talents can be achieved. Cecelia Frances Page continues to write more, worthwhile books to inspire her readers.

Fiction

ONE

Tasper the Ghost

Tasper the ghost could come and go wherever he wanted to go day or night. Tasper could fly around into houses and into high-rise buildings. He felt free as a bird to move around to many places.

Tasper the ghost was able to float visibly and invisibly. Sometimes people could see him and sometimes they weren't able to see him. Tasper appeared where he could observe children playing and where adults were having adventures and fun.

Tasper did not try to scare anyone who saw him float around. Tasper was a friendly ghost. Tasper liked to talk to children and friendly adults. Tasper watched several children playing in a park. They were playing on a long slide. As they slid down the long, twisting slide the children felt the warm sunshine and then a cool breeze occurred.

Tasper suddenly appeared before the children. Jerry, Wilma and Jerome saw Tasper flying by. They were startled to see a ghost appear before them. Tasper went down the slide. He smiled at Jerry, Wilma and Jerome and they sensed that he was friendly.

Tasper said, "I'm having fun on this slide." Then he laughed. Jerry, Wilma and Jerome realized that they didn't have to be afraid of Tasper. They began to relax and accept Tasper because he was pleasant.

Jerry asked, "Who are you? Tasper replied, "I am Tasper the friendly ghost. Who are you?" Jerry replied, "My name is Jerry." Jerry pointed to Wilma and Jerome. He said, "This is Wilma and Jerome, my friends."

Wilma asked, "Where do you come from Tasper?" Tasper smiled at Wilma. He was floating around near Wilma, Jerry and Jerome. Tasper replied, "I come from invisible space." Jerome laughed and asked, "What do you mean by invisible space?" Tasper answered, "It is a special, parallel space I can go to. I can become invisible when I go to this invisible dimension."

Jerry, Wilma and Jerome watched Tasper bounce up and down on the slide. He also continued to float around freely. He appeared energetic and happy. Jerry was curious and he asked, "Can you teach us to float around like you do? "

Tasper floated near Jerry. He took Jerry's hand and Jerry began to float in the air. Jerry was amazed that he could float in the air. Jerry kept floating. He felt light and freer than he had ever been in his life.

Wilma and Jerome watched Jerry floating. They became excited and were amazed when they saw Jerry floating. They wanted to float, too. Tasper took Wilma's hand. She began floating with Tasper's help. Jerome was guided by Tasper. He began to float around.

Jerry, Wilma and Jerome enjoyed floating around in the park with Tasper. They felt free and happy to float around like liberated spirits. Tasper had helped them become freer than they had ever been. Tasper continued to float around near them for at least an hour.

Then Tasper disappeared suddenly as quickly as he had appeared to Wilma, Jerry and Jerome. They looked around for Tasper. Wilma, Jerry and Jerome landed back on the ground safely. They wished Tasper would appear again. Maybe Tasper would reappear again some time.

Cecelia Frances Page

Fiction

TWO

Beyond the Horizon

Sylvester Brown liked to experience adventures. He was eager to go beyond the horizon to find out what was happening. He watched the sunset with its beautiful array of bright colors of red, pink, orange and yellow.

When the summer came the weather was warm and pleasant. Sylvester decided to travel beyond the horizon across the ocean in a big, two, cabin boat with a motor. He navigated with a male friend, Harold Smith. He stayed in the first cabin and Harold stayed in the second cabin.

Before leaving, Sylvester and Harold packed the boat with food such as fresh fruit, vegetables, bread, eggs, cereals, milk, frozen meat and fish plus nuts, beans, rice and honey, etc. They put warm bedding in the cabin beds and brought enough comfortable clothes, shoes and warm jackets. They also brought swim suits and suntan lotion in order to avoid sunburns.

Sylvester and Harold departed from San Diego Harbor early in the morning just as the sun was coming up. The sun was gleaming on the ocean. Sylvester and Harold prepared their breakfast on the boat. Sylvester boiled four eggs. Harold poured cereal into two bowls. He poured milk into the cereal bowls. Then he put honey into the cereal and milk. Sylvester placed two boiled eggs in one dish and two boiled eggs in a second dish.

Sylvester and Harold sat down on the deck of the 20 foot by 14 foot boat to eat their eggs and cereal. They observed the rippling movement of the ocean. Sunlight continued to sparkle on the ocean. The boat was traveling further across the ocean. Seagulls hovered over the boat. They were looking for food. Some of the seagulls landed on the deck of the boat. They observed Sylvester and Harold eating. The seagulls were hungry and they wanted to be fed.

Harold found some bread in the storage area of the cabin. He brought the bread to the deck. He broke the bread into crumbs. Harold threw bread crumbs to the seagulls. They quickly snatched up the bread crumbs as he kept throwing more bread to them. More seagulls landed on the deck. They also ate bread crumbs. Harold and Sylvester finished their breakfast.

While the boat kept moving across the ocean Sylvester and Harold were busy looking after the boat. They checked the sails which would be used when the motor wasn't running. They checked the rudders and hoists. They cleaned the deck after the seagulls flew away. They had messed up the deck.

Sylvester and Harold were headed south to Baja California. They navigated in the ocean near the coast of the long peninsula. They passed Tijuana and Ensenada. They continued past Cabo Colnett. It was getting dark. The moon came out after a brilliant sunset of red, orange, purple and yellow hues of colors. Sylvester and Harold prepared the evening meal. They cooked fish, cut potatoes, and cut fresh tomatoes, carrots and dark green lettuce. Harold prepared a salad with vinegrette dressing. Sylvester fried the cut potatoes and fish. Harold cut some bread with butter.

Harold and Sylvester sat down to eat their fish, potatoes, salad and bread with butter. For dessert they ate some organic chocolate cookies. They drank prepared lemonade. While they ate they observed the moon move across the sky. The moon became very big and bright. Harold and Sylvester studied the stars.

After dinner Sylvester played his guitar and sang popular songs. Harold listened intently. Both of them sang songs together for an hour. Then the two men went to their cabins to rest until morning. The boat was anchored first for the night.

The next morning the sun came over the horizon in the East. Sunlight beamed on the boat. Sylvester woke up first. He got up and prepared some coffee. He decided to get up. It was time for breakfast. As usual the two men prepared their breakfast.

Harold and Sylvester sat on the deck and ate scrambled eggs, hash browns and toast. They drank orange juice. Then they sipped their coffee. After breakfast the anchor was lifted. The boat began moving south again near the Baja Coast.

The boat moved towards Punta San Antonio and then on to Punta Blanca. Sylvester and Harold observed beaches and some palm trees along the Baja Coast. They continued to Santa Rosalia and continued on until they reached Punta Eugelia. It was mid day. Harold and Sylvester hadn't eaten since breakfast time which was approximately 4 hours ago. So, they anchored the boat. Suddenly, a school of dolphins jumped up in the air from the ocean. Sylvester and Harold enjoyed watching the dolphins jumping up in the air.

Harold prepared hamburgers by frying hamburger patties with celery and some seasoning. The cooked hamburger patties were placed between hamburger buns with mustard, catsup, lettuce, pickles and onions. Harold fried more cut potatoes. Harold and Sylvester sipped root beer while they ate their lunch.

After lunch, Sylvester and Harold continued their journey. They traveled past Punta San Pablo to San Juanico. When they came to La Purisima they anchored the boat. Sylvester and Harold decided to go swimming in the ocean to cool off and to exercise. The ocean felt fairly warm because of the piercing sun. Sylvester and Harold swam around. They encountered more dolphins. The dolphins were friendly. Sylvester was able to get on a dolphin's back. The dolphin moved swiftly in the ocean. Sylvester was worried about getting back to the boat because the dolphin moved quite a distance from the boat. Sylvester needed to get back to the boat. He didn't want to swim back. There may have been sharks in the water.

Sylvester fell off of the dolphin's back suddenly. He had no choice. He would have to swim back to the boat. He began swimming. He would have to swim at least a mile to return to the boat. So, he kept swimming. After half a mile of swimming, Sylvester began to become very tired. He kept swimming until he became too exhausted.

Sylvester saw Harold in the distance. Sylvester called to Harold who had lost track of him. Harold finally saw Sylvester in the distance. He swam towards him. He kept swimming until he came up to Sylvester. By then, Harold was also tired.

Harold and Sylvester managed to dog paddle in the ocean while they tried to restore themselves before heading back to the boat. Harold held onto Sylvester. They both swam towards the boat. It took awhile to reach the boat.

Suddenly, several sharks spotted Harold and Sylvester. The sharks headed in their direction. Sylvester saw the sharks. He told Harold about them. Sylvester and Harold began swimming faster. They were trying to get back to the boat before the sharks could harm them.

Finally, Sylvester and Harold reached the boat. They managed to climb up on the boat just in time. The sharks swam close to the boat. Several sharks bumped against the boat. Fortunately, Sylvester and Harold were safely on the boat by then. The sharks would have to go somewhere else for food.

Sylvester and Harold rested in their cabins for hours to recover from their ordeal in the ocean. They had a very narrow escape from death. Hungry sharks usually chose their next meal whenever they can find it. Sylvester and Harold were grateful to be alive and unharmed.

Harold and Sylvester continued towards the tip of the Baja peninsula. For over 500 miles the coastal scenery was mostly deserts. They arrived at huge swamps and lagoons in the Magdalena area with dense, green vegetation. The boat sailed further south to the colorful village of Todos Santos a few miles from the Tropic of Cancer. It was now less than 100 miles from the tip of Baja at Cabo San Lucas. The weather was much warmer because they had come to the southern region of Baja California where average winter days were in the 70s or 80s.

At Cabo San Lucas there are beaches with luxury hotels along the coast. Harold and Sylvester sat on a nearby, pristine, sandy beach to rest. They put suntan lotion on to avoid sun burns. The sun was beating down on the warm beach. The ocean on this southern coastline was much warmer than on the west coast of Baja California.

Sylvester and Harold had journeyed over a thousand miles to reach Cabo San Lucas. A huge, famous, scenic rock separates the Pacific Ocean from the Gulf of California at the tip of the peninsula. Cabo San Lucas is famous for its great diving, surfing, swimming, fishing and yachting. This city is the most popular Baja California tourist resort and the huge cruise ships destination.

After Sylvester and Harold rested on the warm, pristine beach they walked into one of the hotel resorts near the beach to have their dinner. They sat at a table on the outdoor terrace overlooking the beach and scenic ocean. Large, red clay vases with tropical, verdant-green plants were displayed around the terrace.

A server dressed in a colorful, long dress came over to Sylvester and Harold's table on the terrace. She handed them menus. She also served tall glasses of water with sliced lemon. She waited for Harold and Sylvester to select their choices on the menu. Harold and Sylvester studied the selections on the menus.

Harold decided to order lobster with scalloped potatoes, a green salad and seafood chowder. Sylvester ordered large shrimps with a baked potato with cream and chives. He ordered a green salad and clam chowder. They also ordered lemonade. The server went back into the hotel to place the orders. Meanwhile, Sylvester and Harold sipped their ice water with lemon slices. They gazed at the beach and view of the ocean. They observed other boats and ships in the harbor.

Finally, the server brought soup and salad to Harold and Sylvester's table. She placed the soup and salad on Harold and Sylvester's table. She also brought oyster crackers. Sylvester and Harold began tasting their soup. Then they ate their salad. Harold put oyster crackers in his chowder. The server brought the main course of lobster and shrimp.

Harold pulled lobster meat out of the lobster shell. He spread a lobster sauce on the lobster meat. He tasted the scalloped potatoes. Sylvester tasted his shrimp. It tasted delicious. Then he mashed up the baked potato and put sour cream and chives on the potato. Harold and Sylvester enjoyed their dinner. It was the first meal they didn't have to prepare on their boat. The food was very delicious. For dessert Harold had an ice cream sundae. Sylvester had a piece of chocolate cake with a scoop of vanilla ice cream. The two men sipped coffee after their dinner was eaten.

Sylvester and Harold walked around in the hotel lobby and the hotel grounds. They walked past a swimming pool. The water in the pool was turquoise because of the turquoise reflection from mosaic stones. The swimming pool was large. Sylvester and Harold wanted to go swimming in the pool. However, they were not guests of the hotel. So, they didn't attempt to swim in this pool.

That night Sylvester and Harold went back to their boat to sleep in their cabins. The night sky was clear and vivid. Many stars appeared. Venus, Jupiter and Mars appeared closer to the Earth. Sylvester and Harold noticed the Moon, which shone brightly in the sky. The Moon appeared especially large and bright that night. Sylvester and Harold watched the night sky for awhile. Then they fell asleep in their cabins.

Cabo San Lucas had a marina with many boats, sailboats and flaties. Sylvester anchored their boat at the marina. He left the boat with Harold in order to walk around Cabo San Lucas. This magnificent seaport had cobblestone streets and New Orleans shutters. There were terraced gardens with beautiful flowers. Sylvester and Harold appreciated this charming place. Cabo San Lucas had many terracota tiled brown and red roofs on two story homes with stucco walls. Balconies arranged with colorful flowers were displayed so tourists could enjoy their beauty.

The pristine white, sandy beaches were popular. Many visitors walked and sunned themselves on the beach. Some sunbathers sat under thatched umbrellas to shade themselves from the hot, piercing sun. Sylvester and Harold roamed on the beach. They went swimming in the warm ocean.

When Sylvester and Harold returned to their boat, they decided to fish for marlin. They prepared their fishing gear. They stood on deck and cast their fishing rods into the ocean. They waited patiently to catch some fish. They hoped to catch a big marlin. Time went by. The fish were not biting the fish bait.

Finally Sylvester felt a sudden tugging on his fishing rod. He pulled the fishing string in. It was difficult to pull the struggling fish into the boat. Harold helped Sylvester. They both kept trying to pull the fishing line in. A large marlin hooked to the fishing pole, leaped in the air and it fell down into the ocean. The marlin was trying to get loose so it could escape.

Sylvester kept trying to pull the marlin up on the boat. He finally pulled the marlin onto the boat deck. It kept wiggling around trying to breathe. It kept struggling to get away. Finally it stopped moving because it couldn't live long out of the ocean.

The marlin was 12 feet long by 6 feet wide. It was a beautiful, large fish with a sharp point on its mouth. Sylvester had succeeded in catching an enormous fish. His hands were bleeding because of his struggle to catch this large fish. Sylvester and Harold would have many fish dinners because this marlin was so big.

Sylvester and Harold cut up the marlin into portions. They cleaned the cut fish and wrapped all the pieces in plastic containers. They put the fish in the freezer and refrigerator on their boat inside the cabin kitchen.

Sylvester and Harold decided to travel north along the coast of Baja so they could go back to San Diego, in California. They prepared marlin each day to eat up this fish. They prepared potatoes and vegetables and buttered bread. For dessert they ate cake or cookies with cut fruit. They didn't drink coffee at night because it caused them to stay awake.

The boat moved along at 40 miles an hour. Sylvester and Harold returned to San Diego in three days. They still had some frozen marlin left. Sylvester and Harold went beyond the horizon over and over in order to navigate back to their home in San Diego, California.

THREE

Speculations and Answers

We can speculate about why we exist as human beings. Why were we created with souls? What is the purpose for living on Earth? Could we have lived on other planets? The answers to these speculations and questions can be answered. Different religious and spiritual gurus and teachers have given answers to these questions.

Some spiritual teachers have spoken about birth and death. We are affected by the karmic wheel of life and death. Our DNA has been changed by interbreeding with human beings who were more evolved. Human beings were created by Lords and Sons of Fohat. Our souls were created by God, the creator. The spark of divinity was put into our souls. We are affected by physical time which causes us to live and die. We have lessons to learn about life on Earth. The purpose of our existence is to search for our true divinity so we can evolve step by step to serve God and all life we come in contact with.

It is very possible that many human beings were created in races and subraces. There are the yellow, white, brown, black and red races. These races may have come from other planetary systems such as Lyra, the Pleiades, Orion and the Big Dipper and Little Dipper, etc.

More primitive human species became more evolved when their DNA was improved through interbreeding with more evolved human beings. Evolution of the human species has continued step by step.

We can speculate why the Earth was created over 5 billion years ago by breaking away from the Sun. The Earth was a fireball. Eventually, it began to cool off. The Earth was covered with liquid. In time, continents formed. The plant and animal kingdoms were created. People believe that some of the plants and animals were brought to Earth from other planets.

People speculate if there is life on other planets. There are millions of planets in the Universe. Therefore, it is realistic to be aware that the evolution of life forms exist on other planets. Scientists are studying planets in our solar system. Space shuttles have been sent near the moons circling around Jupiter. Water has been discovered and seen on Europa, a moon rotating around Jupiter.

UFOs have traveled to Earth. Extraterrestrial beings have been seen on Earth. Eric Von Daniken, Billy Mier, Zecharia Sitchin, Bill Birnes and others gathered evidence about UFOs and extraterrestrials who came to Earth in ancient times. Evidence has been gathered about UFOs which have been coming to Earth in present times. Eric Von Daniken has gathered writings in the form of ancient tablets, rock carvings, ancient statues and alien skulls.

We should keep an open mind in order to learn all we can about controversial topics and issues. Many speculations can be resolved so that humanity can seek answers to previously, unknown issues.

Nonfiction

FOUR

Continue Being Creative

Creativity is an ongoing experience. It is worthwhile to maintain a creative mind and lifestyle. Creative thinking inspires individuals to be productive persons. Composers, artists, writers and architects are creative individuals. They tend to pursue their creative talents.

Composers who continue to compose new songs, sonatas, polonaises, operas, operettas and orchestra arrangements are experiencing new melodies and accomplishments. They hear and write down what sounds they are able to compose. Artists sketch original drawings of landscapes, seascapes, portraits, still life and geometric designs. Artists use a blend of oil and water colors. Lighter colors blend with darker colors. Perspective is used so viewers can look into the paintings and sketches. Artists are able to reproduce realistic images on canvasses with paint brushes and charcoal pencils.

Writers are able to write original poems, plays, short stories, articles, original reports and theses. Writers are capable of writing original ideas that can inspire and stimulate their readers. A writer who continues to write original novels, nonfiction, short stories and articles continues to be a creative thinker. Great writers have helped to change the world.

Architects came up with original architectural designs. Modern buildings, homes and other structures designed by architects change the appearance of cities and towns. Unique, architectural structures add to the beauty of different environments.

Creative individuals have made a difference in the world. Their creative achievements have added to world cultures. Appreciation for the Creative Arts extends around the world. Many people enjoy worthwhile art work, music, literature and beautiful architecture. Continue to be creative in order to feel a sense of achievement. You will help change the lifestyle of others by adding your creative awareness.

FIVE

Dubai—A Modern Country In the Middle East

The tallest building in the world today is in Dubai in the Middle East. Dubai is a clever blend of unique architecture. Dubai is a small emirate which turned into a Middle East financial giant.

"Lacking the oil reserves of the emirate's neighbors, Dubai's ruling family created a parallel economic reality fueled by real estate, international investment and the art of the possible. The emirate was fashioned into a sleek cityscape of startling images", said Jeffrey Fleishman and Merris Lute.

The world's tallest building went up. The Dubai Airport never closed. The Burj Dubai, the tallest building in the world, shines in Dubai in the United Arab Emirates. However, the recession has left the emirate with miles of office space it can't rent.

"Dubai was the first Arab city that proved to the world that it could compare to a Western city with its buildings and its vision", said Randa Habib, Jordanian, political analyst.

Dubai is one of the seven emirates that make up the United Arab Emirates, a nation wedged between the Persian Gulf and Saudi Arabia. The UAE's Central Bank has offered emergency support to banks with holdings in Dubai. The neighboring emirate, Abu Dhali, which has rich oil reserves, is expected to offer a limited rescue to keep the crisis contained.

Collapsing real estate values were not the visions of Dubai's ruler, Sheik Mohammed Ibn Rashid of Maktum, whose goal was to build an international city that would echo the grandeur of centuries past, when Baghdad and other capitals symbolized the power of the Islamic world.

After Dubai emerged from British control in 1971, its ruling family quickly turned to finance, opening an airport, creating free trade zones and reaching into regional markets.

Sheik Maktum was a poet and an equestrian. He was guiding much of the development before he was named ruler in 2006. His book, MY VISION urged other countries to follow Dubai's success.

The emirate's architecture, with buildings that billowed like sails or twirled in delicate angles," personified the rising confidence and influence of Persian Gulf nations. Dubai's style challenged Arab world stalwarts such as Egypt and attracted a younger generation of Arab professionals from filmmakers to accountants.

Dubai drew a wave of new languages. About 85% of Dubai's population of 1.7 million are from other countries including about 250,000 construction, most of them from India and elsewhere in Asia. Dubai is improving its economy. However, Al Qaeda and the Taliban along with drug smugglers and gunrunners have taken money in Dubai's financial institutions, according to U.S. investigators.

Nonfiction

SIX

Cabin Homes on a Cruise Ship

200 homes are being built on a $1.1 billion cruise ship which is set to cast off in 2013. The business plan is to sell half the cabins as floating homes.

Opulent cabins aboard the ship Utopia now range in price from about $3.7 million to $26 million. During the Cannes Film Festival, the ship is slated to drop anchor near the south of France, in the Mediterranean Sea. During the carnival celebration in Rio de Janeiro, the ship plans to dock off the coast of the Brazilian city. On New Year's Eve, cruise ship operators hope to take passengers to Sydney Harbor in Australia to enjoy the fireworks display.

David Robb, chairman of Utopia Residences, has a model of the Utopia. Utopia Residences have a model of the Utopia. Utopia Residences Company placed an order last month with Samsung Heavy Industries to build the 971 foot, 105,000 ton ship, scheduled to launch from South Korea. Once completed, the Utopia will offer 204 cabins that can be rented like hotel rooms for limited periods. An additional 200 cabins will be sold as permanent residences, with prices ranging from about $3.7 million for a 1,400 square foot home with two bedrooms and two bathrooms to $26 million for a 6,600 square foot cabin with four bedrooms and three bathrooms.

Utopia officials say purchasers would be buying a cabin on the ship but not an ownership share of the ship. In addition, the cabin owners would have to pay regular fees for utilities, security, concierge services and access to private onboard clubs.

Some of the cabins feature hardwood floors, marble kitchen countertops, recessed lighting, walk-in closets and fireplaces. Owners and renters would have access to the ship's many amenities, including three swimming pools, tennis courts, an outdoor movie theater, a miniature golf course, shops, restaurants and a "lazy river" meandering around the deck.

Utopia will cruise the seas coming to port so passengers could enjoy the world's most celebrated sporting and cultural events. Among the events on the utopia itinerary are the Tour de France bicycle race, the Monaco Grand Prix car races and the Americas Cup yacht race.

Wealthy individuals with a lot of money can afford to buy or rent a cabin on the Utopia. They will be able to enjoy many luxuries plus travel around the world to see many exciting and beautiful, scenic places.

SEVEN

Hatchback Five-Door Electric Ford

The hatchback, five-door, Ford Focus is displayed during a preview for the world automobile media at the North American International Auto Show in Detroit. The automaker also wins car and truck of the year awards at the Detroit Auto Show.

Ford Motor Company announced its intentions to sell an all-electric version of the vehicle starting next year. Ford Motor Company said the electric version of the Focus would be built at a factory in Michigan that previously manufactured sport utility vehicles, which Ford President of America, Mark Fields observed was an example of how quickly the auto industry and consumer tastes were shifting.

The price will be competitive with other electric vehicles such as rival Chevrolet's Volt. GM hasn't announced pricing for the Volt, either.

The electric vehicle will be built alongside the next generation Focus, a compact car that Ford sees as a key part of its strategy to leverage global design and engineering to produce a vehicle that will sell well in many global markets.

"The new Focus will be nearly identical in all markets with 80% parts commonality around the world. The efficiencies generated by our new global C-car platform will enable us to provide Ford Focus customers with an affordable product offering quality, fuel efficiency, safety and technology beyond their expectations," said Alan Mulally, Ford's chief executive.

The Focus will come in both four-door sedan and five-door hatchback styles. Production will start in Europe and North America in 2010 and sales are expected to begin early in 2011.

Nonfiction

EIGHT

What Are Animals Aware Of?

In recent years scientists have discovered that certain animals and dolphins are far more aware than formerly realized. For instance, monkeys have been trained to operate computers. One example is an experiment where a variety of food was clicked on a computer screen by a monkey using a computer mouse. The monkey learned that if it clicked on the proper sequences, using the proper computer keys, and chose a picture of a banana it was rewarded with that fruit. If the monkey clicked on a vegetable that monkeys refuse to eat it would fail to get what it desired. Monkeys were also able to click up photos of different species of monkey and primates and other animals. They are able to move the mouse to the monkey they choose on the computer screen and click on. Monkeys have also been taught to do rapid and complex mathematical computations on a computer.

A pet owner may wonder if a cat or dog can perceive and enjoy beautiful symphony music on a living room stereo or TV program. If loud, jerky, screaming, angry punk, rap or heavy metal music is played what would dogs and cats think or feel? Would pets react to music the same way as humans? Would these animals have different personalities like different humans? Many people love the types of rock music that other people hate. So, would a different cat prefer a song that another cat can't stand?

Cecelia Frances Page

It is well known that different cats and dogs have radically different personalities from each other. Pets of the same species differ in traits like being energetic or lazy, friendly or fearful, shy or aggressive, protective or apathetic, loving or angry, rough or gentle in how they get along with other pets. These distinctions are often seen in the same household. Some pets change their moods dramatically when they react while others maintain the same personality. Some pets don't mind riding in cars while others are scared and freak out.

A cat can also prefer or reject the *same* diet of other cats. One cat was observed totally refusing to eat popular, gourmet, menu fish, meat and cheeses from a highly rated restaurant. This cat would "only" eat packaged, formula, synthetic cat crackers! When offered other forms of packaged or canned cat food the animal refused with a disgusted expression. This cat insisted that all of its meals were exactly the same one-course, repetitive crackers. However, another cat that was this cat's friend would eagerly eat all the restaurant food it was offered.

For many years consumers and researchers believed that pigs, cows and various other ranch animals were so dumb and unemotional that they could be treated like slaves, harshly handled and raised in disgusting conditions by human standards. In the late 20th Century tests revealed these livestock were far more intelligent, aware and emotional than believed. The animals had all of our human emotions. The livestock could sense their coming execution and became very stressed and sad. The animals had severe depression when their children or family was taken away. Yet, the livestock were treated like items on a production and manufacturing assembly line, with no compassion from owners. The animals were regarded as disposable, economic commodities, raised only for profit and with no concern about their feelings, thoughts and comfort.

An amazing discovery was that cows, pigs and sheep had the same emotions as well-treated horses. Pigs were found to be one of the most intelligent animals. There were reports of pigs that were found to be as smart as many popular pets. However, pigs were discriminated against and used only for food and profit.

Humans have many illogical and contradictory ideas and prejudices regarding animals. In America, Europe and Australia dolphins are regarded as nearly as intelligent as humans, great friends, and so emotionally and psychically advanced that they should never be used for food. However, in Japan dolphins are a popular food.

People are prejudiced regarding dogs and horses which are popular restaurant and home meals in several nations. This menu is found to be disgusting by most Americans and Europeans. People who consume dolphins, dogs and horses have no compassion for their superior intelligence, awareness and emotions. However, most Americans and Europeans eat animals of equal intelligence and emotions. The only reason for this paradox is habit, tradition and a lack of awareness of the human feelings of these animals.

Researchers have also found that different animals of exactly the same species have different levels of intelligence like humans. A dog, cow, horse and pig can have a much higher I.Q. than a relative of the same breed. Many animals can also be trained to be more creative, alert, obedient, disciplined, athletic, proficient and productive as they grow older. This form of advancement is the same as with humans!

At circuses and arenas animals have been trained to compete in races, games and acrobatic contests. Do the winners of these sports events feel pride and egotism at winning and humiliation and depression in defeat? Dogs have clearly demonstrated pride in their accomplishments and can whine and look sad when they are scolded or fail.

One of the most remarkable examples of the great intelligence and awareness of an animal species was researched in Germany at the beginning of the 20th Century. A horse named Clever Hans was taught how to add, subtract, multiply and divide numbers. This horse was able to count, perform simple reading and tell the date of the week. Clever was also able to demonstrate the difference between different types of music.

The method of horse mathematics and reading was done by the different directions and sequences when the horse struck bowling pins. The results were placed on a blackboard in front of the horse.

The different bowling pins represented different numbers and letters. The pins could also represent music chords.

Demonstrations of these events were verified by Professor Edward Claparede of the University of Geneva, Switzerland. This researcher had studied a group of horses in Germany that demonstrated how to calculate square roots and cube rates of numbers up to seven digits. The professor did research with Wilhelm von Osten who had taught Clever his skills. These same mathematical and reading skills were then taught to two additional horses. The horse learned to spell the names of guests.

A hundred years later Michael Tymn did excellent research on these horses to attain the results. Details were published in *Atlantis Rising* magazine in a highly recommended article.

Monkeys can also be trained to do much of what these horses performed. Cats, dogs and pigs are very intelligent like horses. Could those animals be trained to do mathematics and spell also? This field of science is open for many possibilities.

There are well documented cases of families who moved to another state far away. These people left their pets at the former home. The dogs and cats refused to live without their owners and hiked hundreds of miles through wilderness, cities, mountains, deserts, forests and strange territories to find the new homes. Humans, without maps and directions, would have become totally lost in the same situations! Nobody gave these pets directions, so how could they find one home in a town of hundreds or thousands of homes that is hundreds of miles away?

Steve Omar witnessed an event with his pet cat. The landlord refused to allow the cat outside the apartment. However, this cat loved the outdoors and became extremely angry, resentful and unfriendly if left in the apartment all day. If allowed outside the cat became loving, playful and very friendly.

However, angry neighbors complained that the cat was in their yards and jumped on top of their cars. They demanded that the landlord evict the cat from the apartments. The landlord demanded that the cat be kept indoors 24 hours a day or it would be evicted.

The theoretical solution was for Steve to take his cat to the beach every day. The cat could enjoy playing in the park next to the beach while Steve Omar surfed. However, when Steve returned from surfing the cat totally vanished.

The apartment was over two miles from the beach through a complicated maze of twisting and intersecting streets. The cat had been brought to the beach in a jeep, and it remained on the floor and unable to see out any window. So, there was no way the cat could have known the route to this beach park!

The next day the cat was heard knocking on Steve's apartment door with its paws. At first, the cat was visibly mad at its owner. However, the pet mellowed out after a few hours and became very friendly and loving.

The following day Steve decided to tie the cat to a leash at the beach park so it could not escape. Before leashing the cat it was allowed to walk and run around the park with Steve following. The cat was playing and having a good time. However, when the cat was leashed to a tree while Steve surfed it became extremely angry. When Steve had tried to lock it in the jeep it was even madder and freaked out.

When Steve returned from a brief surfing session the cat had escaped again. The animal was nowhere in sight. Once again it found its away home and knocked on the door.

The cat was no so uptight that Steve decided to sneak it outdoors. However, the landlord chased it with a net and threatened to capture the cat and have it taken to the abandoned pet center. Most pets were executed at that place, so this was unacceptable to Steve.

The next day Steve decided to take the cat to a different beach that was much further away. He took the cat for a long walk and then locked it in the jeep. As soon as the cat entered the jeep in the apartment parking lot it threw a terrible temper tantrum. The cat could obviously predict what was going to happen. The pet kept banging on the windows in a rage and had a terrified look on its face. Steve felt sorry for the cat, but knew that this plan was better than his cat getting kidnapped and killed by the landlord. At least the cat could go for a long walk and play on the beach before it was locked in the jeep.

However, as soon as Steve opened the door at the beach the cat jumped out the opening door and fled like a bullet. The cat was well aware of the plan. Steve never had a chance to grab the cat because it was too fast.

This beach was so far away and the route home was so complicated, that Steve worried his cat would be lost in the wilderness and would never return. However, a few days later the cat arrived at the apartment and knocked on the door!

Since a human could not find a way home under these circumstances, the cat had demonstrated superior awareness. Did this cat have psychic powers? It has also been proven that cats can see things invisible to humans and hear beyond the human range of sounds.

However, the cat had now changed into a different personality. Originally the cat had been extremely loving, cuddly, friendly, mellow, playful and easy to get along with. Now it would sense the time when Steve was going to leave the apartment. The cat now spent most of the time in the apartment up on a high ledge where it was out of reach. The pet would leave the ledge to grab its meal when nobody was close enough to grab it. The cat now refused to be petted or cuddled and appeared fearful and uptight. These are very human emotions and thoughts! The cat would run from Steve whenever he approached.

The cat thought he could outsmart and outrun the landlord. So, he continued to dash out of the apartment whenever a guest or room-mate opened a door. The pet was so fast that he kept going outside. For a few weeks the clever cat always escaped the chasing landlord and became confident he could always get away. The cat became like a clever thief that believes he is so tricky that he will never get caught by chasing police. Eventually the thief makes a mistake and was caught. After many successful escapes the cat finally made a mistake and was caught off guard, captured in a net and taken away by the landlord. Steve never saw his cat again.

Perhaps it is time that all humans begin to treat all animals with the same Golden Rule that they treat their fellow humans and friends. Animals have thoughts, motives, feelings and goals just like humans. Animals should not be exploited and manipulated like the slaves before the Civil War. Treat all animals with respect, dignity, compassion, empathy, care and love.

NINE

Planetoids in Outer Space

Planetoids are asteroids. What is an asteroid? An asteroid is an object that appears like a star from a great distance moving in space. Some are very small planets and most are chunks of rock. Most asteroids in our solar system orbit between Mars and Jupiter in space.

There are many asteroids between Mars and Jupiter. However, more and more asteroids are moving outside the asteroid belt and some are heading in the direction of the Earth.

The largest asteroid is 490 miles in diameter. Hundreds of asteroids were created when Maldek was destroyed. Maldek was a planet which orbited the Sun between Mars and Jupiter. Maldek exploded into many moving fragments and became planetoids or asteroids.

It is very possible that planetoids exist in other solar systems. Planets may have been destroyed in other solar systems. Asteroids are capable of floating around randomly. They could float into outer space and collide with other moving objects in space.

Planetoids are much smaller than planets that move in an orbit between other planets. Some planetoids may have life on them. They may have bacteria and small life forms on them. Some planetoids may merge with other asteroids to form larger planetoids or small planets.

Scientists and astronomers have been observing asteroids moving in the direction of the Earth. Some asteroids may come directly to the Earth to collide on the Earth's surface. This could cause serious problems on the Earth's surface such as severe earthquakes and cataclysms. Life on Earth may be destroyed. Scientists are trying to find ways to prevent asteroids from colliding on the Earth. If the asteroid was far enough away it could be exploded into fragments with missiles. However, this could create a dangerous, small meteors bombardment if the asteroid was close to Earth. The more favorable plan is to land rockets on the asteroid and use their thrusts to steer the asteroid in a different route away from Earth.

Cecelia Frances Page

Nonfiction

TEN

Why We Need to Know God

Why do we need to know God? Many people wonder if God exists. Some people have never even heard about God. Yet, God is a very vital part of our lives. God created each soul in God's image. Every atom, cell and electron is created by God. God is the divine creator of all life.

We should learn to know God in our daily lives. Our lives will have much more meaning if we pray to God. We can become One with God. We can become One with God and all good.

We can pray to God to guide us when we need to overcome emotional problems and challenges in our lives. God is able to help us find peace and harmony in our lives. God can help us realize the purpose of our lives. We will find more meaning and we can become enlightened and illumined because God has given us the opportunity to seek truth, wisdom and knowledge during each Earthly embodiment.

It is up to each soul to know God. During our lifetime we are able to learn as much as we can about the Earth and creations on Earth. God created all living things on Earth. We should become aware of the Cosmic Plan. All life is evolving in conformity with God's divine blueprint. So, make God an important part of your life. Pray to God and meditate every day. Endeavor to research in order to help us all to live better lives. We all need to give thanks to God for all his gifts.

ELEVEN

Scientific Methods

Scientists have developed the scientific method. This scientific method has helped scientists to develop theories and to find evidence and solutions to discover knowledge about nature and space.

What is the scientific method? Steps of the scientific method are as follows. First, select a topic and develop a topic and theory. Second, develop a question or questions to find answers about. Third, go seek answers to the questions. Fourth, gather specific, tangible evidence to prove your theory about the topic. Fifth, state your conclusions to prove your theory.

Scientists have used the scientific method to develop their scientific theories. Sir Isaac Newton developed theories about gravity by observing apples fall to the ground. Other scientists such as Pierre and Marie Curie discovered radium by experimenting in a laboratory. They discovered radium glowing in the dark. Albert Einstein developed the Theory of Relativity. He developed a famous algebra formula E+MC2.

Galileo and Copernicus used the scientific method to discover theories and seek knowledge about our solar system. Galileo used a handmade telescope to discover planets in our solar system. He found out planets including our Earth revolve around our Sun. He proved the Earth was not the center of our solar system by closely observing the Earth's orbit around the Sun. He also observed the Moon orbit around the Earth.

Copernicus discovered the Earth was closer to the Sun at a certain time of the year. The Earth was farthest from the Sun at another time. Copernicus discovered parogee and apogee in regards to the Earth's orbit around the Sun.

Charles Darwin gathered tangible evidence when he went to the Galapagos Islands. He gathered different birds, insects, reptiles and amphibians. He brought his collection of different species back to England. He developed a theory of evolution. He theorized that human beings evolved from the apes and monkeys.

Each scientist has developed his or her own theories using the scientific method. Each scientist developed theories. They searched for answers and evidence to prove their theories.

Nonfiction

TWELVE

What You Need to Know About Yourself

What do you need to know about yourself? Each of us has the opportunity to learn about himself and herself. For instance, you can learn from your personal habits why you feel a certain way. You can evaluate your attitudes and philosophy of life. Why do you think a certain way? Why are some issues, topics and subjects more important to you than other topics, issues and subjects?

Some individuals focus on music or art while other individuals focus on Social Science or Science. Other individuals focus on History or Religion. Each individual focuses on what he or she is interested in. Environment, home life and upbringing have a strong influence in what kind of person each of us become.

You can learn a lot about yourself if you can consciously observe yourself every day. Find out why you react a certain way to situations and specific experiences. Why do you become angry, resentful, unhappy, happy, jealous and fearful about certain experiences in your daily life?

How can you learn to overcome hatred, anger, fear, jealousy, resentment and bitterness? How can you develop self esteem and self confidence? How can you experience success and avoid failure?

To develop self esteem takes positive thinking and the development of an optimistic outlook on life. You need to believe in yourself and learn to trust your philosophy of life. You need to believe in what you are doing in your daily life. You also need to believe in other people to have a meaningful life. We all need other people in our lives so we can relate to them in order to feel we belong.

Ask yourself why you select certain friends? Why do you like certain people more than other people? Why do you react to certain beliefs in a positive way? Why do you react in a negative way about other beliefs? Are you prejudiced about certain lifestyles, racial groups and behavior? If so, why?

You have an opportunity to know yourself? You can evaluate your reactions and behavior on a regular basis. When you learn to understand your feelings and reactions about many experiences in your life you will be able to become enlightened. You can experience self realization and awaken to higher thoughts and worthwhile experiences and actions.

Nonfiction

THIRTEEN

Earthquake Tragedy in Haiti

On Tuesday, January 12, 2010 a severe 7.2 Richter-measured earthquake occurred in Haiti. Over 50,000 people were killed. At least 3 million people were injured. Many people were crushed under buildings that crumbled to the ground.

Several major hospitals were badly damaged. Electricity and running, tap water were shut off because of the severe damage caused by the turbulent earthquake.

5,000 people at a time have needed immediate medical attention. There aren't enough medical supplies. Former President Bill Clinton and President Barrack Obama have asked Americans to contribute money to be used to buy supplies and medical equipment as well as enough food for many homeless people who are living outside on the ground throughout Port au Prince, the major city of Haiti. Towns and villages on Haiti have been badly damaged.

At least 70% of the people of Haiti are suffering because of the lack of enough food, personal supplies and medical aid. More than 50% of the homes and dwellings have been badly damaged. Many people are homeless.

There have been serious fights, and violence among people lingering in the streets in Port au Prince. Policemen have had to stop violence especially among young adults and teenagers. Some homeless individuals have attempted to steal supplies donated by the Red Cross.

Anyone who can donate money should contact the Red Cross in their area. The Red Cross will use the contributions to purchase food, supplies and medical aid to send to Haiti. $21 million dollars have been collected to use for this emergency in Haiti.

It may take four or five years for Haiti to recover from this severe earthquake. Within a week a second earthquake has occurred which measured 6.1 on the Richter scale. More damage has occurred.

People around the world are urged to send donations to help the people on Haiti to recover from this earthquake tragedy. The rubble will need to be cleaned up. Buildings will have to be rebuilt. Hospitals will need to be repaired. It will take millions of dollars to restore Haiti. The homeless people will need new, rebuilt homes and dwellings. The economy has been badly affected. So, the economy of Haiti will need to be restored.

Nonfiction

FOURTEEN

Reading Enrichment

Reading is an important subject. Reading enrichment is worthwhile because individuals can learn a lot about people, places, cultural events, religious experiences, history, scientific awareness and many more subjects.

Reading can awaken readers to vivid descriptions of nature and life. Meaningful memories are revealed. Humorous anecdotes and stories are entertaining and cause us to laugh and recognize humor.

Reading broadens our horizons. We are able to acquire knowledge from a variety of books. We are able to go to the library to select books of our choice. We also may do research about different subjects at the library. We can use reference books such as encyclopedias.

Reading enrichment helps readers learn about many issues, topics and subjects. The more individuals read quality books such as classics in literature, the readers become educated and aware of many ideas and viewpoints when they continue to read newspapers, magazines, journals and worthwhile books. So, continue to enrich your life by reading stimulating books and current events.

Nonfiction

FIFTEEN

Pyramid Power

One of the easiest ways to harness energy fields is to build a pyramid or other cone-shaped structure. Since all physical matter is absorbing and releasing torsion fields in a new model, one can capture and direct these waves by building the right kind of structure. The most effective slope angle for such a pyramid is 70 degrees and no metal should be used in its construction because metal has a tendency to absorb the torsion fields around itself.

Once the Soviet Union collapsed, many highly intelligent scientists had little or nothing to do and because of their background in torsion-wave physics, a variety of pyramid experiments were conducted.

Two step pyramids with 70 degree slope angles were constructed in Russia near Moscow. One was at a height of 22 meters and another at a height of 44 meters (144 feet), costing over a million dollars to build. Since the early 1990s, a total of 17 different pyramids have been built altogether. Modular fiberglass plastics were used to build the pyramids.

The pyramids were aligned to the North Star and built away from populated areas. At the base of the 22 meter pyramid the fiberglass wall was 36 centimeters thick and at the base of the 44 meter pyramid the fiberglass wall was 70 centimeters thick. The 22 meter pyramid weighed a total of 25 tons ands the 44 meter pyramid weighed a total of 55 tons.

Several different teams from the Russian Academy of Sciences carried out all sorts of experiments in these pyramids with surprising results. Some dramatic findings are as follows:

Professor S.M. and D.N. Nasik, M.D.s, from the Ivanvskii R & D Institute of Virology within the Russian Academy of Medical Science, conducted a study involving the drug venoglobulin, which is a naturally occurring virus fighting compound in human beings. When the drug was diluted into a concentration of 50 micrograms per milliliter and stored in the fighting viruses.

Professor A.G. Antonov, from the Russian R. & D. Institute of Pediatrics, Obstetrics and Gynecology, tested the effects of a solution of 40% glucose in distilled water after it had been store in the pyramid. By administering only one milliliter of the glucose to twenty different prematurely born infant patients with compromised immune systems, their levels of health were seen to rapidly increase up to practically normal values. The researchers furthermore discovered that the same effect could be produced by simply using one milliliter of ordinary water that had been stored in the pyramid.

Dr. N.B. Egorova at the Machnikov R. & D. Institute within the Russian Academy of Medical Science tested living organisms for viruses. Sixty percent of them survived in pyramids whereas only 7% survived in the control group outside the pyramids. In other experiments by Egonova, mice were exposed to various carcinogens and an experimental group drank pyramid water. The control group drank ordinary water. The mice drinking the pyramid water had significantly fewer tumors developed than the mice drinking the ordinary water.

Agricultural seeds were kept in a pyramid for one to five days before being planted. More than twenty different seed varieties were planted across tens of thousands of hectares. In all cases, the seeds from the pyramid had a 20 to 100% increase in their yield. The plants did not get sick and were not affected in their yield. The plants did not get sick and were not affected by drought.

Poisons and other toxins become less destructive to living systems after even a short term of exposure in a pyramid. Radio-active materials held inside a pyramid decay more rapidly than expected. Pathogenic viruses and bacteria become significantly less damaging to life after being held in a pyramid. Psychotropic drugs have less of an effect on people either staying inside a pyramid or within close range of a pyramid. Radioactive materials held inside a pyramid decay more rapidly than expected. Pathogenic viruses and bacteria become significantly less damaging to life after being held in a pyramid. Psychotropic drugs have less of an effect on people either staying inside a pyramid or within close range of a pyramid.

A 12 meter pyramid was used to increase the productivity of wheat by 400% in the Ramenskoe settlement of Moscow. Dr.Yuri Bogdanov from the Scientific and Technological Institute of Transcription (TTR), in Kharkiv, Ukraine, discovered that the crystallization patterns of salts change in a pyramid. Concrete became stronger. The half-life of radioactive carbon was shortened. Crystals exhibited different optical behaviors such as becoming clearer. Rabbits and white rats exposed to the pyramid gained 200% more endurance and a higher concentration of white blood cells. Water within or underneath a pyramid is purified. Inside power is very helpful because the energy in pyramids increases vitality and cures diseases.

In 1976, Steve Omar was employed as a researcher for the Pyramid Environmental Systems, Incorporated technology office and factory. There was a scientific research building and laboratory in Van Nuys, California. They developed products involving complex, mathematical technological innovations and utilizations of inter-dimensional, biocosmic energy fields produced by pyramid shaped vortices. These constructions required precise mathematical geometry and the science of triangular geometry.

These inventions were designed to energize and heal the body, eliminate pain, slow down the aging process, rejuvenate the body and enhance alertness. Other products accelerated plant growth and the quality of the vegetation and crops.

It was discovered that pyramids constructed with specific mathematical geometry and components of materials, preserved perishable foods without refrigeration or electricity.

All of these devices consisted of interconnected tubing framework containing pyramid-shaped molecular arrangements in the materials. The tubing could be filled with bionic sand which was composed of pyramid shaped crystals. Fifty-two degree ----diagonals and other mathematical configurations were utilized. These pyramids came in different sizes ranging from about three inches high to large enough to sleep in. Test subjects, who meditated, testified increased psychic powers and expanded consciousness using these devices.

Another device was a magic wand that was a small tube about the size of a large pen that contained bionic sand crystals. Bionic sand contained millions of natural pyramid shaped crystals. The metal tubing had pyramid shaped molecular configurations. These wands amplified cosmic energy.

The Pyramid Matrix Antennae device could be suspended over a bed to improve sleep quality, rejuvenate the body and brain, meditate and slow the aging process. A geometrical pyramid-shaped hat made out these materials could be worn for these results and reported expanded cosmic consciousness or ESP powers.

Vegetables, fruits, dairy products, fish and other perishable foods placed inside one of these small pyramids would preserve the items without refrigeration! The quality of nutrition was reported to be improved. Crops grew faster with improved quality under pyramids. The quality of water was allegedly improved.

Steve Omar's research agency, MIND INTERNATIONAL, developed these inventions under the direction of inventor and owner Nick Edwards. Steve's associate Phil Geiger also utilized certain experiments and innovations developed by Dr. Pat Flanagan, who was then the most famous American pyramid energy researcher and author. This group was in contact with Dr. Flanagan. Steve and Phil invented the Rejuvatron. Over 50 desktop pyramids, about a foot high each and made of these materials and bionic sand, were combined into a long cylinder. The metallic cylinder was connected to a Tesla multi-wave oscillator that amplified energy.

Steve was extremely tired several hours after midnight after working on their International Intelligencer newspaper. This researcher felt like falling asleep. Instead, he climbed into the Rejuvatron and Geiger turned on the energy. Immediately bursts of cosmic energy filled Steve's body and brain. The energy became so intense that Steve had to leave the Rejuvatron feeling too energized and alert. He had enough energy to run around the block of the office neighborhood outside and was unable to get to sleep.

A woman on Maui named Dionne lived in a glass pyramid. When she was about 3 to 38 years old many people who met her guessed she was in her early 20s! She reported enhanced meditation and consciousness.

Fiction

SIXTEEN

The Tea Party

Cheryl Jordan was a very social person. She enjoyed meeting people and making new friends. She was able to communicate readily about a variety of subjects because she was an avid reader. She kept up with current events and she read many interesting books.

Cheryl decided to have a tea party in her backyard. It was late spring and the weather was pleasant. The sun often came out on a daily basis. Cheryl sent out invitations to at least 30 people. She arranged to have the tea party on a Saturday afternoon at 2 p.m. in two weeks on April 24th of the year.

Coffee, tea, cookies, ice cream and sliced, mixed fruit would be served at the tea party. Fancy coffee and tea cups with saucers, plates, forks spoons and napkins would be available at the tea party. Cheryl prepared all of the food, beverages and party supplies. She was eager for the day of the tea party to arrive.

Finally, the day of the tea party did arrive. Guests began to arrive around 2 p.m. They were seated out in the backyard garden as they arrived at garden tables. The garden was beautiful because flowers were blooming. Green grass added to the natural decor of the garden. A few evergreen trees were standing in the garden providing shade in the background.

When everyone arrived and were seated Cheryl began serving tea and coffee. She brought cookies and fruit to each table. The visitors selected cookies and cut fruit to put on their plates which had been set at each seat. Cheryl then brought cake to each table. The cake was already cut.

After everyone was served refreshments at each table Cheryl sat down to serve herself. She observed her guests were enjoying the food and sipping their tea and coffee. The guests began visiting with other guests at their table. Cheryl listened to guests at her table. The sun was shining brightly in the garden.

Cheryl decided to talk about a book she had recently read. The book was entitled ADVENTURES IN ALASKA. Cheryl asked the guests at her table, "Have any of you been to Alaska?" The four other people at Cheryl's table looked at Cheryl. A lady to her right called Barbara replied, "No. But I wish I could go to Alaska!" A lady sitting on Cheryl's left replied, "I have been to Alaska's Airport in Anchorage on my way to Canada. A gentleman called Bob said, "I have been to Fairbanks and Dawson City in Alaska around ten years ago. I would like to go back to Alaska some day."

Cheryl listened to her friends. She spoke, "I have been learning about Alaska from the book I have been reading. I would like to go to Denali National Park. There are a lot of wild animals there to observe." Anna, sitting at Cheryl's right asked, "Who are some wild animals living at Denali National Park?" Cheryl answered, "There are black bears, moose, white foxes, reindeer and wolves. It is very beautiful for at least four months of the year at Denali. I would like to go there. I would like to see the Borealous lights. I have heard that green, white and blue lights flash across the sky."

Cheryl continued to talk about what she read about Alaska to her friends. She was having a good time socializing. Many of her friends didn't read prolifically as Cheryl did. She was able to talk "circles" around her friends. Yet, she wanted to socialize with them.

Cheryl got up and walked around to visit with more of her friends. Some of them were talking about their personal hobbies such as tennis, volleyball and baseball. Others were talking about different foods they enjoyed eating. Some of them were talking about their family life and their jobs.

The tea party lasted for several hours. The refreshments, tea and coffee were eaten and drunk up. The guests began to leave one by one. Finally, the tea party was over. Cheryl planned to have another tea party in the near future.

SEVENTEEN

Revisit Alice in Wonderland

ALICE IN WONDERLAND is a famous, children's classic written in England by Lewis Carroll. We will revisit Wonderland to find out what else could have happened to Alice which was not told in the original story.

Alice fell asleep again and she dreamt that she entered a magical, blissful domain. There were sparkling trees and geometric flowers along a golden pathway. Alice continued to explore Wonderland. She saw beautiful, angelic beings floating around singing celestial melodies. Wonderland was a very pleasant place. The sky was a violet color instead of blue.

Alice saw palaces with golden and white spires around each palace. People came out of the palaces dressed in majestic gowns and masculine attire. The people had golden blonde and red hair. They were graceful and pleasant to observe.

Alice decided to stop at one of the golden palaces. She walked to the entrance to the large, elegant, golden doors. The doors opened as she came close to them. Alice walked into the palace. The walls sparkled and glittered as she walked through the halls. She came to a spacious room which sparkled with diamond light. Angelic beings were floating around. They appeared like heavenly beings.

Alice spoke to some of these angelic beings. They kept singing celestial songs. Alice decided to stay to listen to their celestial songs. These angelic beings sang about the stars in the heavens. They sang about flowers, trees and mountains on the Earth.

Alice was very impressed with the celestial songs which the angelic beings sang so sweetly with their magnificent voices. Alice felt at peace. She also felt safe. She loved this blissful, heavenly place.

Alice wanted to stay longer in this golden palace. Yet, she felt something causing her to leave and to move on to more experiences. So, Alice eventually walked out of the palace. She continued walking along the golden pathway.

Alice came up to a tall, sparkling tree. The tree began to move and sway. Alice was amazed at the trees movements. Then the tree began to speak to Alice. The tree said, "Hello. What is your name?" Alice was startled when she heard this tree speaking to her. Alice decided to speak to the tree. She said, "I am Alice. Who are you?"

The tree had an expressive face. It smiled at Alice and answered, "I am Howard, the friendly tree." Alice responded, "I didn't know trees could talk. How did you learn to talk?" Alice spoke, "I tried to talk to some angels in a palace earlier. They were singing together. Yet, they wouldn't talk to me. They just kept singing."

Howard the talking tree, said, "I talk to anyone who comes by me. Some people talk to me and some other people ignore me and keep walking on. I am glad you stopped to talk to me." Howard smiled at Alice. Alice responded, "Trees don't talk on the Earth. I was very surprised when I heard you speak." Howard laughed and said, "Just call me the talking tree! I'll be here whenever you want to talk to me."

Alice enjoyed visiting with Howard, the talking tree. She said, "Maybe I will come back this way. Nice knowing you Howard. Bye." Alice continued walking on the golden pathway. She came to a sparkling lake. There were white, graceful swans moving on the lake. The lake was a lavender-blue color with sparkling light emanating on it.

Alice sat down near the edge of the lake. She watched the white swans floating along rhythmically on the lake. She was fascinated with their graceful movements. She fell asleep. Then she woke up and she was back on the Earth near her home. She got up and walked home. She went into her house and greeted her parents. Her mother asked where she had been. Alice replied, "I was in a magic land called Wonderland." Alice's mother looked at Alice with an expression of disbelief. Alice's mother responded, "So, you went to a Wonderland. You must have been dreaming!" Alice answered, "If I was dreaming it seemed too real!" Alice sat down in a chair in the living room and recalled her unusual experience in her dream about Wonderland.

Fiction

EIGHTEEN

Imaginary Figures

Imaginary figures danced around a large room in someone's home. These imaginary figures were dressed in purple, gold and white gowns of satin and silk. They moved around gracefully around the lit up room.

The family in the house could not see these imaginary figures moving around in the room. The reason the imaginary figures could not be seen is because they were in another dimension. Yet, they occupied the same location as the people in the house. They were invisible.

The imaginary figures were eager and energetic as they moved around the house. The people in the house did not notice them of course. So, the imaginary figures could do what they wanted to do.

One day seven of the imaginary figures decided to explore some nearby forests. They floated near tall, evergreen fir and pine trees. They were able to see the tall trees. They realized how solid and big the trees were. They even were able to smell the fragrance of the trees. They continued to go around the trees through many branches.

Then the seven figures came to a moving stream. They floated into the flowing water. They didn't get wet because they were in another dimension. Yet, they saw the moving stream. They noticed how the stream moved in a certain direction. They followed the stream until the stream flowed into the ocean.

The seven imaginary figures saw the enormous ocean. They noticed how waves crashed down in the ocean and splashed onto the pristine sand. The sand became wet. Designs rippled in the wet sand. The imaginary figures were interested in the designs made in the sand. No one could see these imaginary figures floating in the ocean and walking in the sand. They didn't get wet or have sand on their feet because they continued to be in another dimension.

The imaginary figures continued to explore around the Earth. They floated to distant places such as Europe and Australia. They continued to notice different places. Yet, no one could see them. They were able to dance at a ballroom where men and women were dancing. No one saw them dancing in the same ballroom because they were invisible.

The seven imaginary figures continued to have fun in their dimension while they saw what was happening on the Earth. They were able to observe the behavior of people. Yet, people were not able to see or hear them. They continued to live in their dimension. Human beings, animals and plants didn't see them or hear them. The imaginary figures could go on doing what they wanted because they were not restricted by time or space. They were happy to move around freely and to live freely.

Nonfiction

NINETEEN

Invisible Reality

Invisible planes exist and are very real. Each soul has seven bodies such as the physical, mental, emotional, astral, I Am Presence, soul presence and Christ Self. The only visible body is the physical body.\

So, how can we become aware of invisible reality? We have an inner, invisible eye which is used to see the lower and higher astral planes where our invisible bodies dwell. We store all our memories in our mental body. We recall every emotion we experience in our emotional body. We can see the lower astral plane by visualizing images of the Earth in our third eye in our pineal gland which is between our two physical eyes.

The higher astral plane is where our three higher bodies exist. We learn to know God because our three higher bodies exist in the higher God planes. These three higher bodies are the soul presence, Christ Self and I Am Presence. All God knowledge, wisdom and truth are recorded and stored in these three higher bodies. Without these three higher bodies we would not be able to recognize God and the planes of divinity.

Invisible reality has always existed. All higher planes which protect us and maintain the divinity of God within each soul are permanent, invisible reality. We can become aware and enlightened about invisible reality when we look within for inner truth, light and wisdom. Through quiet meditation we can recognize God reality. The All Seeing Eye of God can be awakened as we seek invisible dimensions. It should become the goal of all enlightened souls to become aware of the seven bodies each soul has in order to awaken to invisible reality.

Nonfiction

TWENTY

Music in Daily Life

Our selection of music in our daily lives affects how we feel. Music can cause us to experience joy and happiness. Music also affects us by causing us to feel unhappy. Music may cause us to feel moody and even depressed. So, we need to be careful how we select and listen to music.

Classical music is usually in 3/4 or 4/4 time. The piano, harp and other string instruments are played. Different types of classical music are arpeggios, largos, polonaises, etudes, mazurkas, sonatas, preludes, etc. Orchestra music as well as piano or harp solos are presented. Generally, classical music may be relaxing. Some orchestra music may not lift us up.

The classical compositions of Bach, Mozart, Beethoven, Schubert, Debussy Grieg, Mendelssohn, Weber, Chopin, Liszt and others may uplift and relax us as we sit or work around the house. We are affected by the rhythm and sound of this worthwhile music.

Semi-classical music also may help us relax as well as bring emotional upliftment. Broadway hits and songs may cheer us up. We may feel much better because we are enjoying pleasant music.

Music can affect our heartbeat. If unrhythmical, harsh music is played and listened to on the radio and television the harsh sounding music may cause our body rhythm to become imbalanced. It is best not to listen to harsh, unrhythmical music. You will remain healthier if you avoid hard rock and unmusical sounds.

The classical works of Frederic Chopin are very relaxing and healing to the physical, emotional and mental bodies. Chopin composed Prelude in D Flat major "Rain Drops", Prelude No. 2 in B Flat Major", "Piano Concerto No. 1 in E Minor or Romanze Larghetto" as well as many other piano pieces. Franz Liszt composed "Paganini Etude No. 3 "La Campanella." Johannes Brahms composed "Inermezzo in A Minor OP76 No. 7." Peter Tschaikowsky composed "Barcarole" From "The Saisons." Felix Mendelssohn composed "Duetto in F Major. Woflgang Amadeus Mozart composed "Piano Sonata in F Major K 33211 Adagio". Franz Schubert composed "Impromptu In A Flat Major D 899 No. 4". Ludwig Van Beethoven composed "Piano Concerto No. 3 in C Minor." Robert Schumann composed "Einsame Blumen." Alexander Scriabin composed "Nocturne For The Left Hand." All of these classical compositions are wonderful to listen to. These selections should relax you and uplift you.

Relaxing modern hits are "Strangers In Paradise", "Autumn Leaves", "Summertime", "Moonlight Serenade", "True Love", "Fascination", "Night and Day", "Moon River", "Born Free", "Somewhere My Love", "Love Me Tender", "Tammy", "If Ever I Would Leave You", "Camelot", "Vien Rose", "Roman Holiday", "Heather On The Hill", "My Favorite Things", "Trees", "Deep River", "He's Got The Whole World In His Hands", "Somebody Bigger Than You and I", "Be My Love", "Flower Song", "The Loveliest Night Of The Year", "Music To Disappear In", "Music Of The Pleiades" and more.

Nonfiction

TWENTY-ONE

Accomplished Astronomers

Galileo was the first astronomer who discovered that the Earth revolved around the Sun. Galileo created the first telescope. He looked in his telescope at the stars and planets. Galileo discovered different planets. He found out that all the planets revolved around the Sun.

Copernicus continued to study the heavens. He discovered the orbit of the Earth. He found out the Earth is closer to the Sun at certain times of the year. Then the Earth is farther away at other times of the year. He called these distances apogee and parogee. Apogee means the Earth is farthest from the Sun. Parogee means the Earth is closest to the Sun. Copernicus studied different orbits of planets in our solar system.

Carl Sagan was responsible for developing SETI. SETI is Search For Extraterrestrial Intelligence using a large facility with discs attempting to detect intelligent radio signals from other planets. Complex electronic technology is utilized. The main SETI installation is in Puerto Rico.

Dr. J. Allen Hynek was the American Air Force astronomer and scientific advisor for Project Bluebook. That group was the official Air Force investigation into UFOs in the 1950s and 1960s. While working for the Air Force Hynek ridiculed most UFO reports as a public skeptic. However, when this Northwestern University scientist retired from his military work he admitted there are real, mechanical, solid unidentified flying objects made by no known nation on Earth. Hynek concluded many UFOs could be from other dimensions.

Astronomer <u>Harold Wilkins</u> discovered a lot of things on the Moon. He described geological features and concluded there was no oxygen or water on the Moon's surface.

Professor <u>Clyde Tombaugh</u> discovered Pluto in the 1930s and mistakenly believed it is a planet. It is really a much smaller planetoid. Professor Tombaugh was engaged in a classified project to search for small, undetected, natural satellites of Earth. Satellites had military significance.

Astronomers have measured the Moon's size and mass and arrived at a mean density only about three-fifths of that of the Earth and concluded that the Moon has no metallic core like the earth. From the appearance of the Moon's surface astronomers have known that the gravitational pull there must vary from place to place, as it does on the Earth. The mascons (mass concentration) that slightly disturbed the paths of the Orbiters did not surprise the astronomers.

<u>Steven Hawking</u> is a well known astronomer. He developed the Black Hole Theory. For thirty years he claimed that many galaxies have a black hole in the center of each of them. Hawkings said black holes suck in solar systems which contain suns, planets and planetoids.

Steven Hawking eventually decided there are parallel universes. Parallel planes exist. Life which is swallowed up in black holes still exists on parallel planes. They are in another dimension.

<u>Tony Tyson</u>, a modern astronomer has used telescopes around the world to study galaxies fainter than any ever seen before. Tyson is known for designing and building better detectors that are better equipment to record and analyze the light that telescopes collect and focus. Using his skills in both observations and detector technology, Tyson has spent a decade studying the light from distant galaxies. The heart of his research concentrates not on these concentrations

of stars but on how dark matter between ourselves and distant objects can affect the light we perceive. Tyson has become a cosmic detective, an astronomer who deduces enormous quantities of dark matter from a few clues hidden in the faint glow from galaxies near the edge of the visible universe.

Tyson built a better CCD detector. He discovered empty regions which contained faint blue galaxies in great numbers. These galaxies are many billion light years away. We see them as they were billions of years ago.

Vera Rubin was a woman who first firmly established the existence of great amounts of dark matter seriously. Rubin has been the leading expert on dark matter in more familiar spiral galaxies, those that lie much closer to the Milky Way. Rubin is now a leader in the study of how stars move within galaxies. Vera Rubin has long studied the motions of stars in the Milky Way and in other galaxies. Rubin's greatest coup occurred when she used the technique of analyzing starlight colors to measure stellar motions in the outer parts of our own galaxy and in nearby spiral galaxies.

John Dobson is an astronomer who made telescopes to use to observe the heavens. Dobson practices by showing people how to see the stars.

Johannes Kepler discovered the correct shape of the planets' orbits around the sun Kepler was the first to understand that the planets move in elliptical orbits around the sun. Kepler learned about the Copernican theory as a university student. Kepler was taught that Copernicus' notion was that the planets orbit the Sun.

Kepler had a deep feeling that the planets, and still more the Sun, emitted forces that drove the solar system. Kepler established "Three Laws of Planetary Motion." These three laws are, (1)The planets all move in elliptical orbits around the Sun. (2) The planets move more rapidly when closer to the Sun, less rapidly when farther away in accord with a particular mathematical formula. (3) The size of each planet's orbit is related to the length of time it takes to orbit the Sun, in accord with another mathematical formula.

Sir Isaac Newton (1642-1727) discovered the law of universal gravitation and three basic laws of motion. He observed the Earth as well as the heavens.

Margaret Geller of the Harvard-Smithsonian Center for Astrophysics is one of the leaders in the effort to map the universe. Geller worked with Huchra at the Mount Hopkins Observatory, south of Tucson, Arizona. Geller and Huchra used a telescope with a 60-inch reflector to study the galaxies. They observed slices. Geller and Huchra defined each slice as a strip 6 degrees long extending nearly halfway around the sky. The very first slice that Geller and Huchra plotted fully confirmed the void in Bootes.

Geller and Huchra developed a map which includes 6,000 galaxies which are visible in four slices out to distances of 500 million light years from the Milky Way. In 1989 Geller and Huchra discovered the "Great Wall" which represents the largest ordering of matter now known in a universe, a structure bounded only by the size of the region that has been mapped.

Alan Guth of the Massachusetts Institute of Technology has played a crucial role in developing the new inflationary theory of the Cosmos. Guth discovered with a slow transition the early universe would expand, not as Edwin Hubble had found it, but at an enormously greater rate. Because the false vacuum in fact teams with energy, it tends to produce an explosion of space everywhere with more power than anything imaginable on Earth or for that matter, in the Milky Way.

Edwin Hubble (1889-1953) made the distance determinations that allowed him to discover the expansion of the Universe. Edwin Hubble created the Hubble Space Telescope which is used to study galaxies, black holes and novas far away from the Earth. Hubble's Law describes the expanding universe which states "that all distant objects in the universe are receding from us and the speed of recession increases for points at greater distances. This means that if we observe a photon arriving from a greater distance, that photon must have spent more time on its journey and must therefore have originated in a point that is receding more rapidly."

George Gamow (1904-1968) was a Russian born physicist who made important contributions to atomic physics and also predicts the existence of the cosmic microwave background. He put the model for radioactive decay in mathematically correct form and advanced the field of nuclear physics a bit closer to an exact science.

Paul Richards, professor of physics at the University of California at Berkeley is a pioneer in making observations of the Cosmic background radiation. Richards specialized in using infrared measurements to investigate the properties of solid objects.

Andrew Lange of the Physics Department at the University of California, Berkeley, has collaborated for many years with Paul Richards to measure the cosmic background radiation. Richards tried to steer Lange into observing the background in microwaves, some of which do pass through the atmosphere.

John Mather of the Goddard Space Flight Center led the COBE science team that first measured the spectrum of the cosmic background radiation from a satellite orbiting above the Earth's atmosphere.

Albert Einstein (1879-1955), the greatest physicist of the twentieth century, did his most important work during the period of 1904-1916, before reaching his fortieth birthday. He discovered $E=mc^2$, which describes energy. E lies locked within a amount of mass, m. You simply square the speed light, c and m. Multiply that amount by whatever mass you have. Einstein's equation predicts that greater amounts of mass contain greater amounts of energy. $E=mc2$ offered physicists a way---the only known way---to explain the creation of the enormous amounts of kinetic energy that stars require to shine for billions of years. Astronomers have concluded that stars must convert matter into energy.

Hans Bethe, professor of Physics at Cornell University, discovered the carbon cycle of energy production within stars in 1938. Bethe's carbon cycle, the fruit of his search for the secrets of the stars, drew on his knowledge not only of the reactions that occur among nuclei but also of the abundances of different types of nuclei in the stars.

Cecelia Payne, one of the greatest astronomers of the first half of this century, first applied the new theory of atoms and of the spectral lines they produced to reach a momentous conclusion about the elemental composition of the universe. She produced the most brilliant Ph.D thesis ever written in astronomy. Her thesis concluded that stars consist primarily of the two lightest elements, hydrogen and helium.

Leo Blitz and Eugene DeGeus are two experts in studying star forming regions with radio waves. Radio waves are produced by gas and dust about to form stars. But radio waves can penetrate interstellar clouds without being absorbed by the dusty material that shrouds star forming regions. Radio waves penetrating powers arise from the fact that their wave lengths (the distance between successive wave crests), exceeds the size of most interstellar dust particles. As a result, radio waves can pass by dust-particles and barely notice their presence, as an ocean wave will roll unaffected past an obstacle smaller than its wavelengths.

Professor Edwin Salpeter, of Cornell University has made important contributins to the study of star formation and late stellar evolution. Salpeter is best known for his attempts over the past three decades to understand how stars form, but some of his earliest work in astrophysics dealt with a crucial question about stellar aging. Salpeter showed how stars can "burn" their helium. In effect the star discovers that the "ashes" of its chief nuclear fusion—hydrogen burning—are themselves good fuel.

Subrahmanuan Chandrasckhar was an astronomer who showed that objects with a million times the density of water can exist and persist. White dwarfs can support themselves indefinitely against their own gravity through the invisible hand of the exclusion principle. Chandrasekhar showed that each white dwarf is the dying ember of a star, the once-violent center that fused hydrogen into helium and then helium into carbon nuclei. This ember now quietly does nothing but radiate away its stored supply of energy into space, supported against its own collapse by the exclusion principle. Every white dwarf thus steadily though slowly cools and grows dimmer, taking billions of years to fade into invisibility. White dwarf stars exist by the billions throughout the Milky Way.

Cecelia Frances Page

J. Robert Oppenheimer, an astronomer, developed the theory of neutron stars. He published a paper in 1939 entitled "On Massive Neutron Stars" which calculated what would happen to a group of neutrons compressed to enormous densities. Kip Thorne, one of the leading astrophysicists of our era, has called this paper "one of the great astrophysics or our time." A massive star would have to become a neutron star.

The density of matter in a neutron star makes the density in a white dwarf look like a vacuum. At 100 trillion grams per cubic centimeter, the neutron-star density is a hundred million times greater than the density in a white dwarf.

John Flamsteed, a British astronomer, was the first one to develop a record of a supernova. Supernovas produce nearly all of the nuclei save hydrogen and helium. A supernova may be the driving force behind evolution itself. A supernova appears about twice a century and exceeds that of an ordinary star by many millionfold. A supernova anywhere in the Milky Way will shine for a few months' time more brightly than any star in the sky. The Milky Way contains many hundred supernovae that have already exploded but whose light has not yet reached us.

Jesse Greenstein of the California Institute of Technology is an expert on the spectra of the light from stars and quasars. Greenstein's astronomical career has centered on the study of celestial objects through spectroscopy—spreading the objects' light into different colors, each color providing clues to what the objects are made of. Greenstein's astronomical research has ranged remarkably far and wide from pioneering efforts in radio astronomy during the 1950s through studies of red-giant stars and white dwarfs, to theories of what interstellar dust particles are made of and what tends to align them in the space among the stars. Greenstein continues to maintain a lively interest in all areas of astronomy.

Jesse Greenstein worked with Maarten Schmidt, a professor of astronomy at Caltech and staff member of the Carnegie Observatories. They discovered quasars in collaboration.

Tony Readhead, a radio astronomer at Caltech, is a leader in the field of very long baseline interferometry. Readhead was also a pioneer in developing unified theories of active galaxies---theories that hope to explain quasars.

John Conway, the principal investigator of the VLBI experiment in September 1989, carried an impressive responsibility for an astronomer not yet 30 years old. By using Conway's plan of observing at three slightly different frequencies, the VLVI astronomers hoped to achieve far more detail in their observations than a map made at any single frequency could reveal.

Halton Arp, now at the Max Planck Institute for Physics and Radio-physics near Munich, West Germany, has urged controversial theories of quasars on his fellow astronomers for the past 25 years. Like all astronomers, Arp could see only two dimensions: north-south and east-west on the sky. The third dimension, the distance outward from the Earth, must be estimated, not measured. Halton Arp's photograph of the galaxy NGC 1073, printed as a negative to show detail, reveals three quasars close to the galaxy, either because of a chance lineup or because the quasars are close to the galaxy in space.

Ed Stone, was a leader in the United States' effort to explore the outer solar system. Stone was also the principal investigator for the experiment aboard the spacecraft that measured cosmic rays---charged particles moving at nearly the speed of light.

Onneila Sargent and Steve Beckwith use radio waves to examine the surroundings of young stars for possible planet-forming disks of material.

Nonfiction

TWENTY-TWO

Meteors and Meteorites on Earth

Meteorites are smaller than asteroids. Meteorites are floating in space. They travel to the Earth. Some meteorites burn up before they land on Earth. Other meteorites fall to Earth. Generally, meteorites fall to Earth frequently. Some meteorites are very small while other meteorites are quite large. A large meteor fell into Crater Lake over one hundred years ago. A large lake formed where the meteor created a large crater.

Other meteors have fallen around the world on different continents. Meteors carry hard, rocky substances in them. These meteors bring substances to the Earth. Some meteors become part of the Earth's rocks because they are not recognized as meteors from outer space.

Meteors may come from the asteroid belt between Mars and Jupiter. There are many meteors floating around in the asteroid belt. They break away from their moving pattern in the asteroid belt. Then they float in space. Many of the floating meteorites are attracted to the Earth because of gravitational pull.

Meteors tend to burn up when they come into the Earth's atmosphere. Some meteors become meteorites because they become much smaller before they reach the Earth. Meteorites are usually not harmful. However, extremely large meteors could be harmful.

Asteroids are much larger than meteors. Therefore asteroids can cause much more damage and be far more harmful on the Earth's surface.

The word "meteor" comes from the Greek word meteora or meteoras. This term was once used to describe any atmospheric occurrence, such as auroras, lightning, rainbows, etc. Some felt that meteors were a local event and others felt that meteors occurred at the same general distance as the stars.

It was in the eighteenth century that the heights of meteors were first calculated, using two observers at different locations and parallax. By the end of the eighteenth century, accurate data collected by two German students showed that the altitude of most meteors is between forty eight and sixty miles above the surface of the Earth.

Regular meteor showers occur when the Earth, as it orbits the sun, runs into material left behind by sun-orbiting comets. Meteor showers and the occasional sporadic meteor are often best seen after midnight because we are then facing the direction in which meteoroids are colliding with the Earth's atmosphere at high speed. After midnight, the Earth is literally running into the materials, acting as a big dustpan. Before midnight the material has to catch up with the Earth. One can expect to see about six or seven sporadic meteors per hour before midnight under conditions. This number can almost double after midnight.

"The ZHR showers are many meteors moving across the galaxy. One of the best showers year to year is the August Perseids because of the numbers of meteors the observer can see," states Mike D. Reynolds who is executive director of the Chabot Space and Science Center in Oakland, California. You can count on fifty to one hundred meteors each hour. The Perseids are best to observe after midnight and actually closer to dawn. The best times to observe meteor showers vary from shower to shower.

Many meteors move in different constellations each month. Meteors move in the Quadrantids, Rho Geminids, Delta Concrid and Alpha Leonids in January. In February, meteors move across

Aurigids and Delta Leonids. In March, meteors go across Pi Virginids, Beta Leonids, Eta Uirginids and Theta Virginids. In April, meteors move across Alpha Virginids, Gamma Virginids and Lyrids.

In May, meteors move across Eta Aquarids, May Librids and Northern May Ophiuchids.In June, many meteors flash across Tau Herculids, Theta Ophiuchids, Pi Sagittariids, Ophiuchids. In June they cross Bootids and Scuetids. In July, many meteors flash across Alpha Lyrids and Southern Delta Aquarids. In August, many meteors flash through Alpha Cagricornids, Southern Iota Aquarids, Perseids, Northern Delta Aquarids, Alpha Ursid Majorids, Kappa Cygnids and Northern Iota Aquarids. There are meteors which continue to flash in other constellations in September, October, November and December.

Meteorites have been recognized and collected for millennia. Meteoritic iron was used to make tools as early as 4,000 B.C. The Egyptians called these "Heavenly irons" meteorites. In Mecca, Muslim pilgrims found the Hadshar al Aswad or Black Stone. It was considered to be meteorites. Meteorites have been recorded in many other civilizations, including the Japanese, Chinese and the Europeans and the famous 1492 A.D. Enswisheim fall. In the United States alone, at least twenty-two verified building strikes were recorded in the twentieth century.

In the seventeenth and eighteenth centuries people referred to meteorites as thunderstones. They thought these rocks were volcanic in nature and had dimply been struck by lightning. One of the most famous meteorites that is believed to be of cometary origin is Orgueil, which fell in Montauban, tam-et-Garornne, France on May 14, 1864. Orgueil fragments look like pieces of charcoal briquettes used for barbecuing—and are very expensive.

Most of us do not have everyday access to the Earth's polar regions (though a significant number of meteorites have been recovered in Antarctica). Meteorites can become buried, not only from impact, but also from blowing and shifting sand, agriculture, etc. Erosion can change a meteorite making it almost indistinguishable from terrestrial rocks.

The Tucson Ring meteorite is on display at the Smithsonian Institution Natural Museum of Natural History. The Tucson Ring, an Iron (UNGR) Ataxite, Ni'-rich, is sometimes referred to as the Signet or Irwin-Ainsas Iron. The Enisheim meteorite was displayed in a church. French scientists removed some samples for study. The meteorite was eventually moved to the Ensisheim Town Hall.

The largest recorded meteorite fall occurred near Pultusk, Poland on January 30, 1868. A bright fireball was first seen which exploded loudly. Meteorites literally showered the villages to the east of Pultusk. It has been estimated that more than one hundred thousand meteorites fell. Many of them were only a few grams in weight, leading to the term "Pultusk peas."

A major fall of meteorites was on February 12, 1947, in the Sikhate-Alin Mountains, Siberia when thousands of iron meteorites fell, some forming craters as large as football fields. On December 10, 1984, thirty-six meteorites fell in Claxton, Georgia. One of the meteorites, a 1,455-gram specimen, struck a mailbox and knocked it to the ground.

Many meteorites have fallen to the Earth's surface. Meteors have flashed across the heavens for billions of years.

Nonfiction

TWENTY-THREE

The Last Supper

A famous painting exists entitled THE LAST SUPPER. This famous painting was painted by Leonardo di Vinci who carefully painted a scene with Jesus in the center. Each of the twelve disciples was sitting on the same side of the table. Mary Magdalene was sitting to the left side of the table near Jesus.

The colors in this famous painting are basic reds, blues, browns, yellows and somewhat white. Each disciple at this last supper was sharing a last dinner with Jesus. Bread, wine, vegetables and fruit were on the table.

Mary Magdalene may have been one of Jesus' most important disciples. The fact that the image to the left was a woman indicated the possibility that Mary Magdalene was an important disciple and follower of Jesus.

The twelve disciples were dressed in traditional Jewish clothes. Many of them had long, dark hair. This is the only picture painted of Jesus with his disciples. This painting illustrates the last time Jesus and his disciples ate a meal together before Jesus was crucified.

Jesus and his disciples may have been celebrating Passover which was a Jewish celebration. The Jews were able to cross over into the Promised Land. Jesus was sharing bread and wine with his disciples. The bread and wine was shared as a symbol of Jesus' body.

THE LAST SUPPER is one of the most famous and well known paintings in the world. Copies of THE LAST SUPPER have been displayed around the world. This painting has been seen in many churches, art galleries and even in peoples' homes.

Nonfiction

TWENTY-FOUR

What is Missing in the Bible?

During the Dark Ages and the Crusades and before that era, the BIBLE was changed. Emperor Justinian the first Christian Emperor, had quite a lot of information that was eliminated from the BIBLE because he wanted to control the masses.

Reincarnation was accepted by the early Jews. Reincarnation was mentioned in the Old Testament in ancient BIBLES. Jesus spoke about reincarnation when he was on Earth. The early Essenes were aware of reincarnation during earlier times in Israel.

Reincarnation is no longer in Western Bibles because the scribes were instructed by Emperor Justinian to eliminate information about this belief. Emperor Justinian wanted people to believe we only live one time.

The Book of Enoch was eliminated from the BIBLE. Enoch had written about UFOs and extraterrestrial beings from outer space. Enoch described spaceships in his book. Popes and priests decided to eliminate this valuable information.

The Council of Nicea decided to include Roman and Christian principles and religious beliefs in the BIBLE. They eliminated different prophets, gospels and books. Ancient wisdom was eliminated from the BIBLE.

We may think of the twenty-seven books of the New Testament as the only sacred writings of the early Christians. The LOST SCRIPTURES offers an anthology of up-to-date and readable translations of many non-canonized writings from the first centuries after Christ—texts that have been for the most part lost or neglected for almost two millennia.

Some lost gospels were authored by the apostle Philip, James the brother of Jesus and Mary Magdalene. Epistles written by Paul to the Roman philosopher Seneca, Simon Peter which describes the afterlife and an Epistle by Titus, a companion of Paul are missing in the BIBLE. The Gospel of the Nazarenes fell into disfavor with the Christian community. Few Christians in later centuries could read Aramaic. Also, this Gospel's Jewish emphasis was considered suspicious. As a result, this Gospel came to be lost. Jesus was not born of a virgin, but was a natural human being who was specially chosen to be the messiah because God considered him to be more righteous than anyone else.

The Ebionites were a group of Jewish Christians located in different regions of the Mediterranean from the second to fourth centuries. The Gospel of the Ebionites has been kept out of the BIBLE. In fact, this Gospel has been lost.

The Gospel of the Egyptians is another Gospel that has been lost since the early centuries of Christianity. The second-century Clement of Alexandria described conversations between Jesus and a woman named Salome, who discovered Jesus' empty tomb. Eventually Salome became a prominent figure in some circles of Christianity, including those that produced this Gospel according to the Egyptians.

The Coptic Gospel of Thomas was discovered in 1945. This Gospel was discovered in the village of Nag Hammadi, Egypt when it was accidentally uncovered in a jar containing thirteen leather-bound manuscripts buried sometime in the late fourth century. This Gospel of Thomas records 114 "secret teachings" of Jesus. According to some scholars Thomas may be closer to what Jesus actually taught than what we find in the New Testament. Thomas's document was probably written in the second century after the New Testament.

Cecelia Frances Page

The fragmentary manuscript known as Papyrus Egerton 2 contains a non-canonical Gospel that is never referred to in any ancient source and that was, as a consequence, completely unknown until its publication in 1935. The fragments were discovered among a collection of papyri purchased by the British Museum. This collection of papyri came from Egypt and was dated to around 1510 C.E. This unknown Gospel may have been written before the canonical books of Matthew, Mark, Luke and John. Most of them have concluded that it was produced somewhat later, during the first half of the second century.

The surviving remains preserve four separate stories: (1) an account of Jesus' controversy with Jewish leaders that is similar to stories found in John 5:39-47 and 10:31-9. (2) healing of a leper, reminiscent of Matt. 8" 1-4: Mark 1:40-45., Luke 5: 12-16; and Luke 5:12-16; and Luke 17:11-14. (3) a controversy over paying tribute to Caesar, comparable to Matt. 22: 15-22; Mark 12: 13-17; and Luke 20-26; (4) a fragmentary account of a miracle of Jesus on the bank of the Jordan River, possibly performed to illustrate his parable about the miraculous growth of seeds. This final story has no parallel in the canonical gospels.

The Gospel of Simon Peter was known and used as Scripture in some parts of the Christian church in the second century. Its use was eventually disallowed by church leaders. They considered Simon Peter's writings heretical and not written by Simon Peter.

Simon Peter stated in his Gospel that Jesus remained silent while he was being crucified. Joseph took Jesus to his tomb after his crucifixion. Three men blazing with light came to the tomb. They witnessed Jesus ascend and rise into the heavens. Mary Magdalene came to the tomb and saw the stone was open. She walked into the tomb and saw a beautiful, young man dressed in a very bright garment, sitting in the middle of the tomb. Now, Mary Magdalene, a disciple of the Lord, had been afraid of the Jews, since they were inflamed with anger. She listened to the young man say, "Why have you come? Whom are you seeking? Not the one who was crucified? He had risen and left. But if you do not believe it, stoop down to look, and see the place where he was laid, that he is not there. For he has risen and left for the place from which he was sent?" Then Mary Magdalene and her women friends fled out of fear. They didn't reveal who they saw at first.

The Gospel of Mary is preserved in two Greek fragments of the third century, and a fuller, but still incomplete, Coptic manuscript of the fifth century. Mary Magdalene is accorded a high status among the apostles of Jesus. The apostle Levi acknowledged to his comrades that Jesus loved her more than us." Mary's special relationship with Jesus is seen above all in the circumstance that he reveals to her alone, in a vision, an explanation of the nature of things hidden from the apostles.

The Gospel of Mary was divided into two parts. In the first part, Jesus, after his resurrection, gives a revelation to all his apostles concerning the nature of sin, speaks a final blessing and exhortation, commissions them to preach the gospel and then leaves. In the second part, she describes the vision that she had been granted. Unfortunately, four pages are lost from the manuscript. The vision involved a conversation she had with Jesus, who described how the human could ascend past the four ruling powers of the world in order to find its eternal rest.

The Gospel continues with two of the apostles, Andrew and Peter, challenging Mary's vision and her claim to have experienced it. It ends with Levi pointing out that she was Jesus's favorite and urging them to go forth to preach the gospel as he commanded. They are said to do so, and there the Gospel ends.

The Gospel of Philip was almost completely unknown from late antiquity, through the Middle Ages and down to the present day, until it was discovered as one of the documents in the Nag Hammadi Library. It is not a narrative Gospel of the type found in the New Testament, nor a group of self-contained sayings like the Coptic Gospel of Thomas. It is a collection of mystical reflections that have evidently been excerpted from previously existing sermons, treatises and theological meditations, brought together here under the name of Jesus' disciple Philip. They are difficult to interpret.

Throughout much of this work the Christian sacraments, five are specifically named known as baptism, anointing, Eucharist, salvation and bridal chamber. This work was probably compiled during the third century

Other missing scriptures are the Gospel of Truth, the Gospel of the Savior, the Prato-Gospel of James, the Epistle of the Apostles, the Coptic Apocalypse of Peter, the Second Treatise of the Great Seth and the Secret Gospel of Mark.

Missing non-canonical Acts of the Apostles are the Acts of John, Paul, Thecla, Thomas and Peter. Non-canonical Epistles and related writings were the third letter to the Corinthians, correspondences of Paul and Seneca, letter to the Laodiceans, letters of Clement, the homiles of Clement, the treatise on the Resurrection, The Didache and the letter of Barnabas.

Non-canonical Apocalypses and revelatory treatises which are missing from the BIBLE are the Shepherd of Hermas, the Apocalypse of Peter and Paul, the Secret Book of John On The Origin of the World, the First Thought in Three Forms and the Hymn of the Pearl. Missing canons are the Muratorian Canon, the Canon of Origen of Alexandria, the Canon of Eusebius, the Canon of Athanasius of Alexandria and the Canon of the Third Synod of Carthage.

At least 80% was changed in or deleted from the Western Bible. Only about 20% of the six oldest copies of the Bible that have been publicly translated remain in our current WESTERN BIBLE.

Nonfiction

TWENTY-FIVE

A Healthier Way to Eat

It is important to acquire a healthy way to eat. Food should be organic and fresh. Raw vegetables and fruit are healthy to eat. We should eat bananas, melons, pineapples, apples, oranges, papayas, peaches, grapes, strawberries, goose berries, mangos, tangerines, figs, etc. We should eat raw vegetables such as organic carrots, tomatoes, dark green lettuce, onions, green, yellow and red peppers, cabbage, green beans, spinach, squash, zucchini, parsley, asparagus, kale, etc.

Healthier people usually eat smaller portions. They usually eat six small meals a day. This allows the stomach to burn up the calories. People who can burn off excess calories avoid gaining weight. Maintaining one's ideal weight helps one feel more balanced and healthier.

Whole wheat, grains, corn, beans, oats, rye, different types of nuts such as walnuts, pecans, peanuts, cashews and hazelnuts are delicious and healthy to eat. Fiber is important to eat such as from cereals, wheat germ, and sprouted bread. A vegetarian or vegan diet is a healthier than a flesh or artificial, chemical diet. Vegans do not eat meat, fish or dairy products such as cheese, milk, cream, cottage cheese, yogurt, eggs and butter. Vegetarians do not eat meat, fish and poultry. However, they eat dairy products.

To remain healthy it is best to eat organic, fresh as well as raw food. Exercise is important especially several hours after eating. People who eat carefully usually live much longer.

Avoid eating canned goods, frozen foods, greasy and processed foods. Keep fresh foods such as vegetables and fruits in a cool place. Keep them properly washed. Eat fresh foods as soon as possible so they are really fresh before eating them.

Fiction

TWENTY-SIX

Best Friends

Best friends are special because we can trust them and rely on them. We feel close to our best friends. We are able to communicate with our best friends better than anyone else. We are able to share our deepest thoughts and feelings with our best friends.

Myra Sheridan related well, especially with her best friends. She became very close to her best friends Tanya Dexter, Sheila Howard and Sabrina Torres. Myra often went swimming, played tennis and had slumber parties with these special friends.

Myra confided in her best friends Tanya, Sheila and Sabrina. She spoke about her home life, her boyfriend and what her beliefs were. She spoke about her feelings and attitudes about her home life and school life.

Foxtail and Muffin were Myra's pet dogs. Foxtail was a black, cockerspaniel with floppy ears. Muffin was a golden retriever. Myra was very close to her dogs. She felt her dogs were her best friends. They were her companions at her home. Myra allowed her two dogs to lie down on her bed when she was in her bedroom.

Myra depended on her dogs to walk with her when she strolled in the meadows and forests near where she lived. Foxtail and Muffin barked at other dogs and any harmful animals that might cause harm to Myra. They felt safe with them around. She trained her dogs to be obedient and faithful.

Foxtail was five years old and Muffin was seven years old. Myra helped raise them from puppies. Both dogs responded to Myra like she was their mother. Myra took good care of her dogs. She fed them regularly and bathed them at least once a week. Foxtail and Muffin depended on Myra to take care of them. She was their best friend.

Myra continued to confide in her friends, Tanya, Sheila and Sabrina. She told them about private family experiences. For example, Myra spoke about how her parents argued over family matters. Her parents argued about their finances. They also argued about ways of disciplining their children.

Myra left the living room or dining room where she heard her parents arguing. She didn't want to overhear them because it upset her when they were verbally fighting and causing tension and negative feelings. Myra wanted to be close to her parents. However, she didn't feel close to them. She felt closer to her best friends.

Tanya, Sheila and Sabrina listened intently to Myra. They understood how she felt about Myra's parents' behavior. They felt sympathy for Myra about how her parents were arguing. Myra felt that she could reveal her frustrations and feelings to them.

Myra was glad she could communicate with her best friends. She felt happier when she was able to relate to them.

Fiction

TWENTY-SEVEN

Experiences in Classrooms

Experiences in classrooms vary from day to day. Each classroom is different because of the teachers and specific students. Each person in a classroom adds to what happens day by day. The size of the classroom and how it is decorated effects everyone who participates therein. The amount of students and background and experience of the teacher also affects what will happen in a classroom.

A new school year began in Laredo, Texas in early September in 2009. A new teacher, Miss Cheryl Terrell was assigned to Seventh grade English and Reading classes. Each class of students was different students. Each class had at least thirty-five or more students. Cheryl had six different scheduled classes each day. She also had a study period in which she could prepare lesson plans, grade papers and decorate her classroom. Cheryl was assigned to three English classes and three Reading classes. She prepared lesson plans for each English class and each Reading class. She gathered textbooks to use in each class. She had at least three days to prepare her classroom and lesson plans for both subjects.

School began on Thursday at 8:00 a.m. the first week. Cheryl waited for her students to arrive at her first class. She was somewhat nervous because she wasn't sure how they would respond to her.

The first period English class finally arrived. These students walked into the English classroom and sat down where they wanted to. Cheryl stood before them and waited for all of them to be seated. She asked them to come to attention once all the students had arrived. Cheryl welcomed the students. She told them to call her Miss Terrell. She appeared to be self confident and prepared to present the English lesson. She introduced English for seventh graders.

Cheryl presented an overview and stated purposes for learning English. The thirty-seven students remained quiet and they listened to Cheryl present her English lesson. Cheryl Terrell felt more and more secure. Her first period class seemed to be well behaved and enthusiastic to learn English. Second period came next after the bell. Cheryl introduced herself to thirty students once they all arrived. She took attendance as usual. She described the purpose of English and passed out English literature books. Second period seventh graders seemed well behaved. Cheryl presented the first story in the literature book. She asked different students to read orally. Then she asked questions about the story. Different students responded by answering questions.

When the bell rang the second period English students were dismissed to go onto their next class. Third period students arrived. When the bell rang Cheryl took attendance. Again she introduced herself. Again she presented goals and purposes for the English class. By now the classroom had warmed up considerably. Cheryl put on an air conditioner to cool the classroom. She had thirty-nine students. Some of the students were restless and they whispered and talked among themselves. Cheryl had to remind them to listen quietly. She reminded them of the classroom rules.

Cheryl introduced herself to the third period class. She sensed that this third period class was going to be a challenge. She found out that the students were unable to speak English. They were not able to read in English as well. As a result they were unable to listen and understand what was going on in the classroom. Cheryl would have to find a way to teach them about English literature. She would try to help them learn English.

After third period it was lunch time. Cheryl joined other faculty for lunch in the teacher lounge room. She had brought a sack lunch to eat. She walked over to the teacher lounge room to eat her home prepared tuna sandwiches, cut veggies, cookies and thermos bottle of tea. Cheryl became acquainted with other faculty members while she ate lunch. Her lunch break was 45 minutes.

When lunch was over Cheryl walked back to her classroom. She would continue with fourth period. She would teach seventh grade Reading. She introduced herself as usual and she took attendance. She had forty students in this class. Most of the students arrived on time after the bell rang. Cheryl presented the objectives and purposes for Reading. She passed out Reading books. Then she called on students to read orally after she introduced the first story in the textbook. Some of the seventh grade students had difficulty reading orally because they didn't recognize the vocabulary. Cheryl asked questions about the story and meanings of vocabulary in the story.

Cheryl dismissed the fourth period class when the bell rang. She had a study hall period next for 45 minutes. She was able to work by herself since she had no students during this period. She decided to work on a syllabus which she was required to prepare to turn into the principal for her English and Reading classes. She was required to develop long range goals and purposes, short range goals, procedures and materials needed for each subject. This syllabus was due in two weeks.

Fifth period class and Sixth period were next. Cheryl had thirty-five students in fifth period and thirty students in sixth period. Cheryl had a total of 211 students in all of her classes. She would have a lot of student papers to grade as soon as she assigned written work. She continued to refer to her textbooks for English and Reading to write her syllabus for each subject. Cheryl was tired at the end of the day. She went home at 5:30 p.m.

That night Cheryl went to bed early. Her legs were aching because she had been standing along time during class time. As each day came Cheryl continued to teach both subjects. Months went by. Cheryl had completed her syllabus. She turned it in to the principal.

Cheryl became very familiar with her students. Her first and second period classes were well behaved all year long. Many students did well in these classes. She was challenged the whole year with third period and the sixth period classes. These students didn't want to behave. They didn't complete their class work. Cheryl tried to motivate them. She also had to discipline them. She became discouraged because many of these students didn't seem interested in school.

The first, second, fourth and fifth period classes were achievers. They worked hard and turned in their class work. Many of them did well on tests. Cheryl was glad these four classes responded well. Because of these classes she wanted to go on teaching. She enjoyed teaching these four classes. She was able to motivate the students in these classes.

Miss Cheryl Terrell continued to teach junior high school. She taught sixth, seventh and eighth grade students after the first year of teaching. She continued to teach for 40 years. Cheryl taught her students to comprehend literature. She had them find out about authors who wrote the literature. Her students learned to analyze characterization, plots, themes and to understand vocabulary. They learned to summarize different stories. Her English students learned to write original poems, stories and novels. Cheryl Terrell was a successful teacher for many years.

Nonfiction

TWENTY-EIGHT

About Famous Film Stars

<u>Doris Day</u> was born on April 3, 1924 in Cincinnati, Ohio, USA.. She came from German descent. She is 86 years old in 2010. She lives in Carmel, California on a large estate. Presently she takes care of many dogs. She loves animals, especially dogs.

Doris Day owns an inn in Carmel. Dogs are allowed at the Doris Day Inn. She gave birth to a baby boy who she named Terry. She was close to her son while he was growing up. Doris enjoyed being a mother. Unfortunately, her son Terry was killed during the prime of his life.

Doris Day became a superstar in the movies. Some of her films were Glass Bottom Boat, The Man Who Knew Too Much, Man Who Played A Horn, Young At Heart, Touch Of Mink, Pillow Talk and many more films.

Doris Day became a well known singer in the 1940s, 1950s and 1960s. She starred and co-starred in films with Cary Grant, James Cagney, Rock Hudson, Frank Sinatra, Rod Taylor and Gig Young. Doris also hosted <u>The Doris Day Show</u> in the 1960s. She continued to be a successful singer and film star. Many people have enjoyed seeing Doris Day in films.

Doris Day was known as Doris Mary Happelhoff, the daughter of William von Happelhoff, a local music teacher and Alma Sophia

Welz, a housewife. She had two brothers. Doris Day's parents separated in 1932 when she was eight. Her mother continued to raise her. Doris Day attended parochial schools in Cincinnati, but did not graduate from high school.

Doris Day was interested in dance. Both of her legs were badly broken in a train accident when she was thirteen. She discovered that she could sing. At age sixteen Doris Day began working in 1940 as a singer for Barney Rapp, a regional band leader. She changed her name to Doris Day. She also sang with Bob Crosby and the Bobcats and Les Brown and his Band of Renown.

Doris Day married Al Jordan, a trombone player, and they had a son in 1942. The marriage ended in 1943. Doris Day's fame grew during the 1940s when she appeared in YOUR HIT PARADE and sang with Les Brown's band and produced records such as SENTIMENTAL JOURNEY. Eventually Doris Day signed with Columbia Records which lasted for two decades.

Doris Day worked as an actress for Warner Brothers in ROMANCE ON THE HIGH SEAS. She appeared in seventeen Warner Brothers movies. Fifteen of these films were musicals in which Doris Day played with such leading men as Ronald Reagan, Gordon MacRae, Kirk Douglas, Frank Sinatra, James Stewart, Rod Taylor, David Niven, James Cagney, Rock Hudson, and Gene Nelson. In 1956, Doris Day sang "Que Sera Sera" in THE MAN WHO KNEW TOO MUCH. Doris Day acted in PILLOW TALK, LOVER COME BACK, SEND ME NO FLOWERS, THE THRILL OF IT ALL, MOVE OVER DARLING and WITH SIX YOU GET EGG ROLL. The Doris Day Show aired from 1968 to 1973 on television.

Doris Day received a 1959 Oscar nomination. Five Doris Day films received Oscar nominations in other categories. She also received four Golden Globes Awards. Doris Day is in Hollywood's Star Walk of Fame. She released nearly fifty soundtracks and recorded albums. Since her retirement Doris Day has become very active in Actors and Others for Animals and the Doris Day Animal League and The Doris Day Pet Foundation advocates on behalf of household pets.

Greer Garson was from County Down, North Ireland. She was born on September 29, 1903. She became an actress in her twenties in the 1930s through 1980s. She had beautiful red hair, striking blue eyes and she was very beautiful. Her Irish accent was charming. Greer Garson has acted in many films in England.

Greer Garson acted in leading roles in Random Harvest with Ronald Coleman and Goodbye Mr. Chips. She played a leading role with Walter Pigeon in a World War II film. She co-starred with Robert Taylor as a coal miner's daughter. She was a super star for many years in England. She also co-starred with Laurence Olivier in a love story. She was a vocal soloist and she danced well. Greer Garson had real charm and class.

During the personification of Louis B Mayer's ideal of British refinement and beauty, Greer Garson was the queen of MGM during the World War II years. She inherited the mantles of Garbo and Norma Shearer. Therefore, she starred in the most prestigious films produced by the most prestigious studio in Hollywood.

Louis B. Majors had chosen Greer Garson for an impressive cameo debut in MGM's very popular GOODBYE MR. CHIPS produced in England. This role established her screen personality of warmth, good sense and good humor. Greer Garson was the heroine of PRIDE AND PREJUDICE. In RAINBOW HARVEST Garson performed a music hall number. She reverted to her pristine, classy identity.

Greer Garson continued to perform in JULIA MISBEHAVES and SUNRISE AT CAMPOBELLO. She portrayed Eleanor Roosevelt in SUNRISE AT CAMPOBELLO. She played in TWELVE MEN and then in TV dramas such as REUNION IN VIENNA. Greer Garson received the Best Actress Academy Award for MRS MINIVER in 1942. She also acted in MADAME CURIE, about a French scientist who discovered radium. Greer Garson starred in 32 films from 1939 to 1986.

Jeannette MacDonald was an American actress. She was a leading actress in Maytime with Nelson Eddy. She performed on Firestone Theater on television in the 1950s. She was an opera singer. She had a beautiful voice. Jeannette had red hair and she was very attractive. She performed in many films and was a super star in the 1940s and 1950s.

Jeanette McDonald was born on June 18, 1903 and she passed away on January 14, 1965 at age 61. She was born in Philadelphia, Pennsylvania, U.S.A. She died in Houston, Texas, U.S.A. She was active as an actress and singer from 1919 to 1957. She was best remembered for her musical films of the 1930s with Maurice Chevalier in LOVE ME TONIGHT, THE MERRY WIDOW AND Nelson Eddy in NAUGHTY MARIETTA, ROSE-MARIE AND MAYTIME.

During the 1930s Jeanette MacDonald starred in 29 feature films, four nominated for Best Pictures Oscars (THE LOVE PARADE, ONE HOUR WITH YOU, NAUGHTY MARIETTA and SAN FRANCISCO) and recorded extensively, earning three gold records. She later appeared in grand opera, concerts, radio and television. Jeanette MacDonald was one of the most influential sopranos of the 20th century, introducing grand opera to movie-going audiences and inspiring a generation of singers.

Jeanette MacDonald became a tap dancer during her childhood. She imitated her mother's opera records to sing with Wassil Leps. She performed at church and school functions and began touring in "kiddie" shows.

In 1919 MacDonald joined her old sister, Blossom, in New York and she was in the chorus of Ned Wayburn's THE DEMI-TASSE REVUE, a Broadway musical. In 1920 she appeared in two musicals, Jerome Kern's NIGHT BOAT as a chorus replacement and in IRENE, as the second female lead. In 1921 MacDonald played in TANGERINE, as one of six wives. In 1922 MacDonald was a featured singer in a Greenwhich Village revue, FANTASTIC FRICASSEE. She then performed in THE MAGIC RING in 1923. She performed in TIP TOES, a George Gerhwin hit show. Then she played the second female lead BUBBLIN OVER in 1926, a musical version of BREWSTER'S MILLIONS. She landed the starring role in YES, YES YVETTE in 1927. A sequel was NO, NO NANETTE. Her last play she performed in was BOOM BOOM in 1929 with

Cary Grant. She had already played two plays entitled SUNNY DAYS IN 1928 and ANGELA also in 1928.

In the first sound films in 1929-30, McDonald starred in six films, the first four from Paramount Studios. Her first film was THE LOVE PARADE in 1929. She sang "Dream Lover" and "March of the Grenadiers." THE VAGABOND produced in 1930 was a lavish, two-strip, technicolor film version of Rudolf Friml's hit 1925 operetta. She sang "Some Day" and "Only a Rose."

Other films Jeanette MacDonald performed in for United Artists were THE LOTTERY BRIDE in 1930, DON'T BET ON WOMEN IN 1931 and ANNABELLE'S AFFAIRS in 1931. She returned to Paramount for two films entitled ONE HOUR WITH YOU in 1932 and LOVE ME TONIGHT in 1932. In 1933 Jeanette McDonald was in an MGM FILM ENTITLED the CAT AND THE FILLDE. THE FIREFLY in 1937 was McDonald's first solo starring film at MGM with her name alone above the title.

The MacDonald-Eddy team split in 1937 after MacDonald's engagement and marriage to Gene Raymond. She performed in THE GIRL OF THE GOLDEN WEST in 1938. When Jeanette performed in SWEETHEARTS she suffered a miscarriage during the filming. MacDonald and Lew Ayers (Yong Dr. Kildare) co-starred in BROADWAY SERENADE in 1939. MacDonald went on to film in NEW MOON in 1940 with Nelson Eddy. NEW MOON proved one of MacDonald's most popular films. She sang "Lover, Come Back to Me", "One Kiss" and "Wanting You." Jeanette was in BITTER SWEET in 1940, a technicolor film version of Noel Coward's 1929 stage operetta.

Cary Grant was born in Bristol, England on January 18, 1904. King Edward VII was on the throne in England and Theodore Roosevelt was in the White House in America. His real name was Archibold Alec Leach. As a boy, Cary Grant loved pantomimes to escape from his gloomy existence in the dancing world of the theater. Cary eventually performed pantomimes and became an acrobat. He was adopted by Robert Lomas who trained Cary as an acrobat. Cary performed at the Wintergarten Theatre in Berlin, Germany. Cary, known as Archie, learned to stilt walk. He had to sit upon the shoulders of Robert or Margaret Lomas as they paraded up and down on stilts in their comedy routine. Archie also performed in the Pender Troupe in Paris, France.

In 1911 Archie went to New York with the Pender Troupe aboard the Lusitania. He performed at the Hudson Theater. Then Archie performed at the Norwich Hippodrome in Norfolk. He eventually performed at the Prince's Theatre in Cinderella in Edinburgh. In time, Archie performed at the Globe Theater. He performed at the Hippodrome which accommodated several hundred people on the stage and about a thousand in the audience.

Archie Leach, not yet called Cary Grant, began as an actor in Good Times. The run of Good Times ended on April 30, 1921. He then appeared with the Ringling Brothers and Barnum and Bailey Circus, touring the eastern states of America for three months. Archie returned to New York City for a few days before going to Massachusetts and Connecticut to perform for Poli's vaudeville in circuit. They continued to perform in Washington D.C., Philadelphia and Canada and New York.

Jack and Doris Hartman, Tom and Jim Tomas and Archie Leach formed, with a few American recruits, what was now known as the Lomas Troupe. It played on the Pantages Circuit, starting in Spokane, Washington on September 3, 1923. The Pantages tour took the Lomas Troupe from Spokane and Seattle to Vancouver, Tacoma, Portland, San Francisco and Los Angeles. They traveled on to San Diego, Long Beach, Salt Lake City, Ogden in Utah, Denver, Omaha, Des Moines, Iowa, Kansas City and Memphis. The Lomas Troupe continued on to Ohio, Michigan, Missouri, Tennessee and several other states before they wound up in Wilmington, Delaware in November 1924.

Archie Leach was asked to act in Golden Dawn at the Hammerstein Theater. Then Archie performed in Polly. Then he performed in Boom Boom at Casino Theatre in January, 1929 when he was 25 years old. Then he took an important role in A Wonderful Night which was based on Johann Strauss's operetta Die Fledermaus. Archie Leach also appeared in Music in May, Countess Maritzza, Irene and Rio Rita.

By 1930, Archie Leach was offered a main role in <u>Singapore Sue</u>. Finally, Archie Leach changed his name to Cary Grant. He co-starred in <u>This Is The Night</u> with Lili Damita. Then Cary Grant appeared in <u>Sinners In The Sun</u> with Carole Lombard. He also worked in <u>Merrily We Go to Hell</u>. Cary Grant and Randolph Scott co-starred in <u>Hot Saturday</u>. Then Cary began shooting a nonmusical version of Puccini's opera <u>Madame Butterfly</u> with Sylvia Sidney.

Cary Grant was in <u>The Nuisance</u>, a fast moving comedy-melodrama about a pushy shyster lawyer. Cary Grant then played in <u>Woman Accused</u> with Nancy Carroll. He went on to shoot <u>The Eagle and the Hawk</u>, with Fredric March. Cary was in <u>Gambling Ship</u> and also <u>I'm No Angel</u> opposite Mae West. In 1933, Cary made an appearance as the Mock Turle in <u>Alice in Wonderland</u>.

Cary Grant married Virginia Cherrill. They had a turbulent marriage. Cary often was jealous and possessive. He even hit Virginia violently. They were divorced on March 26, 1935. Cary Grant then acted in <u>Sylvia Scarlett</u>. He then went to England to act in the <u>Amazing Quest of Ernest Bliss</u>. He then acted in <u>Big Brown Eyes</u> with Jean Bennett and then <u>Suzy</u> with Jean Harlow. He then played in <u>Wedding Present</u> with Joan Bennett.

Next, Cary Grant worked in <u>Topper</u>. Cary went on to play <u>The Awful Truth</u> and <u>Bringing Up Baby</u>. Cary Grant's acting career was beginning to be well launched especially in the 1950s. He acted in <u>North By Northwest</u>, <u>That Touch of Mink</u>, <u>Philadelphia Story</u>, <u>The Grass Is Greener On The Other Side</u>, <u>Mr. Roberts</u> and more. He became a superstar. He produced movies in the 1960s.

Cary Grant married Barbara Hutton, who was a millionaire. He related well with her son. The marriage didn't last. In time, he met Diane Cannon, who he married. She was considerably younger than him. He became a father in his eighties. Cary passed away at the age of 82. He was loved by many admirers and movie fans.

Nonfiction

TWENTY-NINE

How Television Affects Our Lives

Television has changed the lives of millions of people around the world. Before television came into many homes, parents and children communicated much more because they were not distracted by television. They went to the theater once or twice a week. During week nights families used to sit in the living room to visit, do school work and share hobbies such as music, cards, checkers and monopoly. They read books, newspapers and magazines. They sat around the fireplace and told stories to each other.

Since the 1950s until today television has become important in millions of homes. Parents and children usually spend many hours watching different television programs. They have favorite TV programs. They must share the television when everyone is home. Advertisements usually interrupt the program every five or ten minutes. Some TV programs have no advertisements. If there are ads they come on in the middle of the film or at the end of the film. Advertisements are very distracting. They cause viewers to lack concentration because advertisements have nothing to do with the actual programs.

Some TV programs are worth viewing such as Travelogues, History, National Geographic, Science, Education, Music, documents and quality films. Oscar winning films are usually quite good. Film classics are appreciated. Much can be learned from watching television.

Yet, television shouldn't be the only form of entertainment. There are plenty of other activities such as reading, tennis, volleyball, chess, table games, ping pong, walking, running, swimming, cards, playing musical instruments, singing, hiking, boating and more. A variety of activities will stimulate individuals to live an active, outgoing life. Television should not take over our lives.

Nonfiction

THIRTY

Where is the World's Oldest Temple?

During the Twentieth Century school students were taught that the oldest temples were in Sumeria and Egypt about 4,500 years ago. Many people still believe in that chronology today. However, from 2000 to 2008 there were many published reports of new temple discoveries that are estimated to be from 7,000 to 17,000 years ago.

Temple and underground ruins have been excavated in Turkey that are estimated to be from between 9,000 and 11,000 years old. Other temple ruins were found in the Rocky Mountains that are so old that even the native Indians could not conjecture dates. Some of these amazing ruins of prehistoric temples were found under the Indian Ocean off the coasts of Ceylon and northwestern India. The architecture was part of ruined cities that contained engineering more advanced than most ancient ruins. The archaeologists in these underwater expeditions estimated they were far older than Egypt and Sumeria and perhaps 7,000 years old. Historians testified that they did not know who built these temple cities from a lost civilization. Some metaphysical researchers believed these cities were built by a lost race called Lemurians.

Another monolithic, underwater, advanced and amazing temple was found off the southern coast of Japan. The age of this extremely advanced engineering accomplishment has been dated to at least 9,000 years ago. This temple has been attributed to the submerged continent of Lemuria, which is also known as Mu.

Small, ancient pyramid and megalithic temples have been found in the dense Everglades of Florida, as well as deep in the Amazon jungles. These temples are so ancient that historians were unable to conjecture dates. Maverick archaeologists and explorers like David Childress, James Churchward, George Williamson and others have published books about prehistoric temples found on several South Pacific Islands. These ruins are so old that it was impossible to figure out the dates of origin. There are also ruins of temples on some of the Hawaiian Islands. On Maui, Kauai and two smaller Hawaiian islets are ruins of stone temples. Archaeologists say these monoliths are so old they cannot calculate their era.

In the 1970s some books were published with a photo of a huge, complex, underground city in Turkey. The subterranean city exhibited very advanced and complex engineering. It was estimated this city was so big it could have held 64,000 people! This ruin was not buried in a cataclysm. The city was intentionally built underground. This ruin was so old that historians could not come up with a date.

Another puzzling ruin in Turkey is the Gobekli Tepe, where carbon dating estimated origins were over 9,000 B.C. German archaeologist Harold Hauptmann and Adnan Misic and Eyup Buruk, from a local museum, excavated this site. This temple was discovered by American archaeologist Peter Benedict in the 1960s. However, this explorer was unable to correctly date the ruins located near the Taurus Mountains. Harold Hauptmann's exploration in 1995 concluded the prehistoric date. Circular, oval and pillar structures were uncovered. Another excavator, Klaus Schmidt believed Gobekli Tepe was the oldest temple in the world.

In 1958 British archaeologist, James Mellaart, found ruins in Turkey that he dated as far back as 7500 B.C. The engineering and architecture was as advanced as cultures that existed over 5,000 years later. Many of the stones used in these ruins are heavier than most of those used to build Egyptian pyramids.

However, the oldest temple ruins estimates have been given to Tijuanaco in Bolivia. Explorers, geologists and archaeologists who have done the most thorough research of this monolithic, temple complex estimated it is up to 17,000 years old.

A remarkable fact about all these prehistoric temple ruins found around the world, that are dated over 7,000 years old, is the extremely heavy and monolithic stone masonry. The engineering indicated that the people who designed these temples, that are now underwater and on land, shared a similar culture of masonry. Many of these extremely ancient temples show a much more difficult, precise and advanced form of engineering than the famous civilizations that arose thousands of years later, in school history books.

All of these temple ruins and prehistoric cities appear to have been destroyed in immense cataclysms. There are dozens of reports of other surviving, undated, prehistoric, monolithic temples in remote Himalayan valleys. Some of those ancient temples are reportedly still utilized by Buddhist priests and monks.

In conclusion, ruins of temples and communities with advanced engineering have been excavated that are over twice as old as attributed dates of ancient Egypt, Sumeria, Babylonia, Greece and Biblical cultures. There is no known, verified, publicized written records of the builders of these lost civilizations. Until recently, conventional historians believed that only primitive, crude, backward, wild cavemen and nomadic tribes lived in the years attributed to these temples. Future excavations may reveal the hidden truth about our ancestors of prehistory.

Nonfiction

THIRTY-ONE

Weather Conditions in the World

Weather conditions vary in the world. The upper hemisphere is much colder during December through March than the southern hemisphere. There is snow and rain in the northern hemisphere winter and temperatures go below zero in various zones.

The weather below the equator varies from hot and humid in the tropical zones to below freezing at sea level in Antarctica, southern Chile and Argentina and in some regions of Tasmania. Temperatures drop far below zero in Antarctica where the South Pole is located. There are several months when there is much less snow and ice. There are lakes and thousands of pools of water. Antarctica is larger than Europe. There are very cold wind storms.

Cold rain occurs frequently along the upper West Coast of the United States in Oregon and Washington states. The northern states in the plains and northeast get severe snow storms in late fall, winter and early spring. Even the Gulf Coast and Mid-Atlantic states may get low temperatures in the 30s and below freezing. The weather becomes colder in Canada and Alaska as well as Greenland, Iceland and the Arctic Circle where the North Pole is located. Upper Europe and Asia become very cold with ice and snow in autumn, winter and early spring. However, most of the United States and the central and eastern portions of Canada get very hot and humid in summer. Hot summer temperatures occur in southern Europe.

There have been many hurricanes, also called typhoons, in the Pacific Islands in tropical latitudes. Hurricanes have occurred in the Caribbean Islands, tropical Atlantic and Gulf of Mexico mainland, and the eastern and gulf coasts of the United States. These regions include parts of Mexico and Central America as well as the Bahamas. Southeast Asia, Japan, Australia, India and Central Africa have experienced hurricanes.

The temperature has been increasing which is causing global warming around certain locations in the world. El Nino in the ocean has caused more frequent rain in affected areas. This condition is far warmer than usual ocean temperatures due to a major change in the location and direction of ocean currents. The warmer climate has caused many glaciers in the Arctic Circle and Alaska to melt to raise the water in the oceans.

The world's climate has continued to become warmer. Global warming continues because of air, water and earth pollution. Man made pollution needs to be stopped so the weather will improve.

Nonfiction

THIRTY-TWO

Life in the 19th Century

Life in the 19th Century from 1800 to 1899 A.D. was a time when inventions were taking place. It also was a time when people were moving west in America to develop more population in the Midwest to the West Coast.

Women were not allowed to vote. The majority of women stayed in the home to raise large families and to do domestic chores. Many women had long hair which they wrapped up on their heads. They wore long neck blouses, long skirts and long dresses. Hats were worn when they went out.

Many families attended church on Sundays. Church picnics, bazaars and folk dancing took place. People traveled in Canastoga wagons and stagecoaches to the West. Horses were used to travel on. Regular wagons pulled by horses were often used.

Men were in control and stated the way of life in the work force and even at home. Women were subservient to men.

Western towns and villages were small with few stores. Every town had blacksmiths to shoe horses. Supplies were purchased at mercantile stores. Fruits and vegetables were brought to small grocery stores by local farmers. There were many farms and ranches.

One room school houses existed in the 19th Century. Teachers were not paid much. Women teachers generally were not allowed to marry while they were teachers. Grade One through Grade Eight were taught in the same room by one teacher. McGuffey Readers were used. The focus was on the three Rs-Reading, Writing and Arithmetic. Geography was taught. Children were taught folk songs. They were taught about God in the one room schools.

Discipline was adhered to in the schools. Rulers were used to spank hands. Teachers had the authority to use physical punishment. Many children walked to school.

The 19th Century was a time of expansion and growth in America. Inventions such as the Bell Telephone, electric light bulbs, Whitney Cotton Gin, oil street lamps, commercial weaving, sewing machines, radios and miscellaneous household items were discovered. Musical instruments such as the piano, violin and guitar were important to learn to play.

Families entertained in their homes. They performed musical instruments and sang folk songs. Folk dancing was also performed in the towns, villages and cities. Streetcars and horses were used in the cities. Television and the film industry had not come into existence yet. Families spent more time together in the evenings. Many people lived on farms and ranches. They had many chores to do every day. They rested on Sundays and attended church and church socials. House raisings and house warmings were popular events.

Few women went to college in the 19th Century. College was reserved for men who usually had money. Women were busy raising families. Some women read a lot and a few women wrote books and stories, such as Louisa May Alcott, Elizabeth Barrett Browning and Jane Austin. Women were allowed to become governesses and housekeepers.

Women sewed most of their clothes, knitted garments and croqueted hankies, towels and scarves. Many women washed clothes by hand. They hung the clothes up to dry on clothes lines. Pot belly stoves were used to heat homes and to cook food. Women worked very hard in order to take care of their families.

Men worked many hours as farmers, ranchers, laborers, bankers, storekeepers, blacksmiths, teachers and ministers, etc. Men worked

16 hours a day six days a week. They rode horses and went in wagons to work.

Families read books around the fireplaces or pot belly stoves. Lamps were used with kerosene or oil. Families communicated around the dining room tables and in the parlors. Children were expected to obey and respect their parents.

THIRTY-THREE

Louisa May Alcott, A Well Known American Writer

Louisa May Alcott was born in Germantown, Pennsylvania on November 29, 1832 which was the same day her father was born. Her father was 33 years old on November 29, 1832. Louisa was a lively, temperamental child. Louisa was active, sentimental, practical and energetic. Louisa had a dark olive complexion and dark gray eyes. Louisa looked like her mother's relatives, the Mays, who may have descended from Portuguese Jews.

Bronson Alcott educated his daughters at home, teaching them to think about what they had learned. Louisa learned at an early age that women were capable of independent thought and action.

Wild Louisa was a tomboy who befriended neighborhood boys only after she had beaten them in a running race. She had no interest in girls who did not like to run or climb trees. She said, "I always thought I must have been a deer or a horse in some former state, because it was such a joy to run."

In 1840 the Alcott family moved to Fruitlands, which became a settlement for 16 people. Charles Lane was a strict leader at Fruitlands. Everyone became vegetarians. They planted potatoes, carrots, turnips, beans, corn, wheat, barley and rye in the fields.

Apple, cherry and peach trees promised abundant fruit. The Alcotts experienced communal living.

Louisa was an enthusiastic reader who read <u>Oliver Twist, The Vicar of Wakefield</u> and many more books. Louisa learned to write in a journal about her personal experiences.

Louisa's mother eventually was the only woman living at Fruitlands. She did all the housework with her girls. The men wrote articles for <u>The Dial</u>, lectured and recruited new members, Abba, Louisa, their other and other girls brought in the harvest of barley, rye and wheat at Fruitlands during torrential rainstorms. Charles Lane, Bronson Alcott and other men were in New York City recruiting new members.

In January 1844 Charles and William Lane left Fruitlands for a Shaker community. The Alcotts packed their belongings and moved to the nearby community of Still River. The Fruitlands Society had lasted just seven months.Louisa wrote a satirical story called <u>Transcendal Wild Cats.</u>

During her teen years, Louisa began to write with a frantic pace that she maintained for the rest of her life. Abba and Bronson Alcott visited several societies, looking for a place to live, work and raise their girls. The following winter the family returned to Concord to be near Ralph Waldo Emerson.

Abba Alcott came into a sum of money willed to her by her father, who had died in 1841. With this sum of money and a large donation from Emerson, the Alcotts were able to buy an old house near Emerson's home which they named Hillside. Located on Lexington Road, Hillside was a colonial structure in disrepair. Louisa developed a lifelong passion for nature in the Concord countryside. Louisa felt this new home had everything she loved---a patch of forest for exploring, meadows for running and a brook for swimming.

Louisa May Alcott grew up from twelve years of age to womanhood at Hillside in Concord, Massachusetts. Bronson Alcott was unable to get a job as a teacher because of the scandal at the Temple School in 1836. People did not think Branson was a suitable educator.

For income, the Alcotts continued to depend on loans and donations from friends, small payments from Abba's inheritance and money from boarders who lived from time to time at Hillside. Bronson worked for Emerson which contributed some money to the family.

Emerson respected Louisa's interest in writing and he let her borrow books from his extensive library. Louisa began to write stories and poems. She wrote fairy stories and romantic thrillers and created adventurous plays she performed with her sisters. Louisa said, "I will do something by and by. Don't care what; teach, sew, act, write, anything to help the family, and I will be rich, famous and happy before I die, See if I won't!"

When Louisa was thirteen she was able to have her own room. She wrote in her diary, "I have at last got the little room I have wanted so long and I am very happy about it. It does me good to be alone. My work-basket and desk are by the window and my closet is full of dried herbs that smell very nice." Louisa's first-floor room had a door that opened onto the garden so Louisa could run out into the woods whenever she liked.

Henry David Thoreau served as an inspirational model for Louisa. Anna and Louisa taught school and worked as governesses or seamstresses. May went to school and developed her artistic talents. Lissie stayed home and kept house. Abba became a social worker. By April 1850 she gave it up for good. Louisa continued to work toward her family and easing their chonic financial problems. In 1850 she gave it up for good. Louisa continued to work toward her family and easing their chronic financial problems. In 1850, Louisa wrote, "Seventeen years I have lived and yet so little do I know, and so much remains to be done before I begin to do what I desire,---a truly good and useful woman," which she wrote in her journal.

Louisa wrote her first novel when she was seventeen entitled THE INHERITANCE. Surrounded by poverty Louisa wrote of a wealthy British family who befriended a poor but lovely and talented, Italian orphan. The setting was a beautiful, English manor. Louisa imagined a world of wealth and beauty far removed from the family's sparse Boston apartment. This book was published in 1997 after her death.

Louisa grew to love city life in Boston, Massachusetts. In 1850, Louisa earned money from her writing for the first time. She sold her first short story, "The Rival Painters" for $5.00. A magazine called the OLIVE BRANCH published anonymously in May 1852. A year earlier she had published a poem, "Sun light" under the pen name Flora Fairfield in PETERSON'S MAGAZINE. In 1852, another story called "A Masked Marriage" was published in DODGE'S LITERARY MUSEUM. Louisa was paid $10.00.

In 1851, Louisa went to work at a private home in Dedham, Massachusetts. She was employed as a companion to older family members. She did hard labor such as lugging water and chopping firewood. She was mistreated by her employers and returned home after she could no longer bear the degrading work. Louisa wrote a tale about her work titled "How I Went Out To Service." It was published twenty-five years later by INDEPENDENT. James T. Field had rejected this story and concluded that she was no writer.

The Alcott sisters staged plays in their dreary Boston apartment. Anna and Louisa dreamed of becoming professional actresses. Louisa believed she could make more money acting than writing. For Louisa, acting was a joyful, creative outlet that temporarily let her forget that she and her family were "poor as rats and apparently quite forgotten by every one but the Lord."

In 1852, a famous author of the Scarlet Letter, Nathaniel Hawthorne, purchased Hillside—the home the Alcotts had owned in Concord. The money from the sale allowed the family to move out of the Boston slums and into a small house in a comfortable neighborhood known as Beacon Hill. Anna and Louisa opened a school and Abba took in boarders.

In 1853, Bronson Alcott lectured to eager audiences in the Midwest; but with little financial gains. For the next four years, Anna and Louisa continued to teach, sew and look after children, often working away from home and living with their employers. In the summer of 1853, Louisa took a job as a servant in the home of a relative in Leicester, Massachusetts. This experience was far better than her first domestic job in Dedham. Domestic work and sewing took up valuable time from her writing. Louisa knew how much her family needed her wages. She never married. Instead she continued to work to support her family and to write.

Louisa May Alcott eventually wrote LITTLE WOMEN which was published in 1868. She then wrote LITTLE MEN which was published in 1871. Louisa's job at Merry's Museum, a popular nineteenth century children's magazine, provided her with a steady income.

Despite her busy schedule, Louisa found time to act in charity plays around the Boston area. The plays disrupted her writing time. She expected to earn $1,000 in 1868 from her writing. She paid bills with most of this money. She helped her sister, May become established as an Art teacher in Boston and she sent money home to her parents in Concord.

With the publication of LITTLE WOMEN, thirty-six year old Louisa became a world famous author. Louisa's ability to write realistic stories and characters earned her the title, "The Children's Friend."

The next twenty years brought Louisa May Alcott success as well as sorrow and sickness. Although she had accomplished her life's goal, she had paid a high price and she knew it. She had settled the Alcotts' debts and made her family secure. During the last eighteen years of her life, Louisa wrote and published twenty-seven books, mostly for children, including EIGHT COUSINS, ROSE IN BLOOM and UNDER THE LILACS. She also wrote countless magazine articles and stories. A children's book entitled OLD FASHIONED GIRL sold 12,000 copies in advance and 27,000 copies within one month of its publication in 1870. Each year, Louisa's publishers reprinted thousands of copies of her novels. Louisa was earning thousands of dollars a year---more than enough to support her family comfortably with funds left over to invest for the future.

When Louisa May Alcott passed away on March 6, 1888, very shortly after her father's death at the age of fifty-five, she was buried on "Author's Ridge" in Concord, Massachusetts at Sleepy Hollow Cemetery close to Ralph Waldo Emerson and Henry David

Thoreau's grave sites. Louisa May Alcott had become a well known and very successful writer. Above all, she sacrificed for her family by supporting and protecting them.

Nonfiction

THIRTY-FOUR

Alternative Energy

Everyone is becoming concerned about the need for alternative energy today. What are some types of alternative energy? There are wind turbines, solar panels, biofuels and geothermal sources. The Central Coast, in California may have a chance to be the forefront of the newest alternative energy known as wave power.

The concept of generating electricity from the motion of the ocean is not new. Offshore devices would use the rising and falling waves to generate electricity, which would then be transferred along a submarine power cable to an onshore station tied into the electrical grid. The power would be then conditioned, usually by storing it in batteries and then sent into the grid.

In December 2009 Pacific Gas and Electric filed for a preliminary permit with the Federal Regulatory Energy Commission to begin a pilot program in the waters off of Vandenberg Air Force Base. The goal is to test the viability of a commercial wave energy project. The program would be similar to P.G. & E. project in Humboldt County.

The Vandenberg project would begin with an environmental study of the waters up to approximately three miles off the coast between Point Arguello and Point Conception.

"Swells from the north and south could potentially provide renewable energy around the clock." Potential is key. While wind and solar play a role in P.G. & E.'s renewable energy portfolio, environmental factors can diminish their power output at times. No wind or no sun means no power. The stretch of coast in question, however, is rarely calm.

P.G. & E. first started investigating wave energy in 2004. The company was told that investigating wave energy might be worth its while. Roger Bedard is the man who told the energy giant about, well, the wave of the future. Bedard's dream was that our nation America would investigate alternative energy. He said, "We've looked at just about every energy source, except ocean energy, which is a huge resource right off our coast."

Bedard worked with P.G. & E. to get the ball rolling on wave energy research and their efforts are coming to fruition with the pilot program in Humboldt County. The project may culminate in a five year, five megawatt study off the coast of Vandenberg.

The topography of the ocean floor, the different ecosystems in place, the offshore and onshore environment will be studied. Because this is such a new technology, the potential environmental impact is being ascertained. Local environmental groups expressed optimism about the concept of wave energy.

"The environmental community is supportive of clean energy," said David Landecker, executive director of the Santa Barbara Environmental Defense Center." The center's concern was about the over industrialization of the ocean," Landecker said.

"The restricted waters off Vandenberg may help matters. There are appropriate uses of the ocean. We're an available market and a willing buyer," said Vandenberg's energy manager, Bradley King, referring to the role the base would play in the project.

According to the memorandum of understanding between P.G. & E. and the Vandenberg Base, Vandenberg would be a direct purchaser of the power generated from the wave project.

Another alternative energy source is the use of solar panels for green power at home. Not long ago, people who wanted to generate their own green energy at home had to content themselves with rooftop solar panels. New technologies and hefty government subsidies are now allowing homeowners to tap the wind, the Earth and other renewable sources in their own backyards. The cost of heating and cooling with fossil fuels has nowhere to go but up, thanks to rising global demand and increased regulation of carbon emissions. It is cheaper and easier to use solar panels to produce green energy to make a clean mini-power plant in one's home.

Approximately 10,500 small wind turbines were sold to the American homes, farms and businesses nationwide in 2008, according to the American Wind Energy Association. A survey of small-turbine manufacturers has projected a thirty-fold increase in the U.S. market by 2013. In Palmdale, city officials are allowing businesses to install wind turbines up to 60 feet high. Among them is Wal Mart Stores, which has as 17 turbine project planned for its Sam's Club store in Palmdale.

California leads the nation in using photovoltaic panels to generate clean electricity. A cheaper and more practical way to harness the sun's energy is for heating water. Solar water heaters typically require just a few small roof top panels. They work even in chilly, northern climates. Officials are hoping to change that with subsidies to coat consumers to swoop their old energy sucking water heaters for efficient solar-power systems.

Nonfiction

THIRTY-FIVE

Laws of Nature

The Vedic scriptures, written in India, declare that the physical world operates under one fundamental law of maya, the principle of relativity and duality. God, the Sole Life, is Absolute Unity; to appear as the separate and diverse manifestations of a creation. He wears a false or unreal veil. That illusory dualistic veil is maya. Many great scientific discoveries of modern times have confirmed this simple pronouncement of the ancient rishis.

Newton's Law of Motion is a law of maya. "To every action there is always an equal and contrary reaction, the mutual actions of any two bodies are always equal and oppositely directed." Action and reaction are thus exactly equal. "To have a single force is impossible. There must be and always is a pair of forces equal and opposite."

Fundamental natural activities all betray their mayic origin. Electricity, for example, is a phenomenon of repulsion and attraction. Its electrons and protons are electrical opposites. The atom or final particle of matter is like the Earth itself, a magnet with positive and negative poles. The entire phenomenal world is under the inexorable sway of polarity. No law of physics, chemistry or any other science is ever found free from inherent opposite or contrasted principles.

Physical science cannot formulate laws outside of maya, which is the very fabric and structure of creation. Nature is Maya. Natural

Science must perforce deal with nature. In her own domain, she is eternal and inexhaustible. Future scientists can do no more than probe one aspect after another of her varied infinitude science. Science remains in a perpetual flux, unable to reach finality; fit to discover the laws of an already existing and functioning Cosmos but powerless to detect the Law Framer and Sole Operator. The majestic manifestations of gravitation and electricity are, no mortal knoweth. Marconi said, "The inability of science to solve life is absolute. The mystery of life is certainly the most persistent problem ever placed before the thought of man."

"To surmount maya was the task assigned to the human race by the millennial prophets. To rise above the duality of creation and perceive the unity of the Creator was conceived of as man's highest goal. Those who cling to the cosmic illusion must accept its essential law of polarity: flow and ebb, rise and fall, day and night, pleasure and pain, good and evil, birth and death. This cyclic pattern assumes a certain anguishing monotony after man has gone through a few thousand human beings. He began then to casting a hopeful eye beyond the compulsions of maya," stated Yogananda.

To remove the veil of maya is to uncover the secret of creation. So long as man remains subject to the dualistic illusions of Nature, the Janus-faced Maya is his goddess. He cannot know the one true God. Among the trillion mysteries of the Cosmos, the most phenomenal is light. Unlike sound waves, whose transmission requires air or other material media, light waves pass freely through the vacuum of interstellar space. Even the hypothetical ether, held as the interplanetary medium of light in the undulatory theory, may be discarded on the Einsteinian ground that the geometrical properties of space render unnecessary a theory of either. Under either hypothesis, light remains the most subtle, the freest from material dependence, of any natural manifestation.

In the gigantic conceptions of Einstein, the velocity of light, 186,300 miles per second—dominates the whole Theory of Relativity. He proved mathematically that the velocity of light is, so far as man's finite mind is concerned, the only constant of a universe in flux.

Einstein developed the Unified Field Theory. He embodied in one mathematical formula the laws of gravitation and of electromagnetism. Reducing the cosmical structure to variations on a single law, Einstein has reached across the ages to the rishis who proclaimed a sole fabric of creation known as a protean maya. On the epochal theory of Relativity have arisen the mathematical possibilities of exploring the ultimate atom, Great scientists are now boldly asserting not only that the atom is energy rather than matter, but that atomic energy is essentially mind-stuff.

"The stream of knowledge," Sir James wrote in THE MYSTERIOUS UNIVERSE, "is heading toward a non-mechanical reality. The Universe begins to look more like a great thought than like a great machine." In his famous equation outlining the equivalence of mass and energy, Einstein proved that the energy in any particle of matter is equal to its mass or weight multiplied by the square of the velocity of light. The release of the atomic energies is brought about through annihilation of the material particles.

Light velocity is a mathematical standard or constant not because there is an absolute value in 186,300 miles a second, but because no material body whose mass is infinite could equal the velocity of light.

This conception brings us to the law of miracles. Masters who are able to materialize and dematerialize their bodies and other objects, and to move with the velocity of light, and to utilize the creative light rays in bringing into instant visibility any physical manifestation, have fulfilled the lawful conditions. Their mass is infinite.

"Let there be light! And there was light." In the creation of the universe God's first command brought into being the structural essential known as light. On the beams of this immaterial medium, occur all divine manifestation. Devotees of every age testify to the appearance of God as flame and light. "His eyes were as a flame of fire," St. John tells us…."and his countenance was as the sun shineth in his strength" which is in Genesis in the Western <u>Bible</u>.

A yogi who through perfect meditation has merged his consciousness with the Creator perceives the cosmic essence as light (vibrations of light energy); to him there is no difference between the light rays composing water and the light rays composing land. Free from matter-consciousness, free from the three dimensions of space and the fourth dimension of time, a master transfers his body of light with equal ease over or through the light rays of earth, water, fire and air.

"If therefore thine eye be single, thy whole body shall be full of light." Long concentration on the liberating spiritual eye has enabled the yogi to destroy all delusions concerning matter and its gravitational weight. He sees the universe as the Lord created it; an essentially undifferentiated mass of light.

And God said, "Let us make man in our image, after our likeness: and let them have dominion over the fish of the sea, and over the fowl of the air, and over the cattle, and over all the Earth, and over every creeping thing that creepeth upon the Earth" which is stated in Genesis in the Bible. For this purpose were man and creation made: that he should rise up as master of maya, knowing his dominion over the Cosmos.

Paramahansa Yogananda was the first great master of India to live in the West for a long period (over thirty years). In his book entitled AUTOBIOGRAPHY OF A YOGI he explains with scientific clarity the subtle but definite laws by which yogis perform miracles and attain self mastery. AUTOBIOGRAPHY OF A YOGI has been translated into twelve languages. Yogananda is a graduate of Calcutta University.

THIRTY-SIX

India's Great Scientist and Inventor Jagadis Chandra Bose

Jagadis Chandra Bose was the first one to invent a wireless coheren and an instrument for indicating the refraction of electric waves. This Indian scientist did not exploit his inventions commercially. His revolutionary discoveries as a plant physiologist are outpacing even his radical achievements as a physicist.

Yogananda admired Bose, who was a handsome, robust man in his fifties, with thick hair, broad forehead and the abstracted eyes of a dreamer. The precision in his tones revealed the lifelong, scientific habit.

The Bose crescograph has the enormousness of ten million magnifications. The microscope enlarges only a few thousand times, yet it brought vital impetus to biological science. The crescograph opens incalculable vistas.

Yogananda said, "You have done much sir to hasten the embrace of East and West with the impersonal arms of science." The telltale charts of my crescograph are evidence for the most skeptical that plants have a sensitive nervous system and a varied emotional life. Love, hate, joy, fear, pleasure, pain, excitability, stupor and countless other appropriate responses to stimuli are as universal in plants as in animals."

When the Bose Institute was opened, Yogananda attended the dedicatory services. Enthusiastic hundreds strolled over the premises. Yogananda was charmed with the artistry and spiritual symbolism of the new home of science.

The work carried out in the Bose laboratory on the response of matter and the unexpected revelations in plant life, have opened very extended regions of inquiry in physics, in physiology, in medicine, in agriculture and even in psychology. Problems hitherto regarded as insoluble have now been brought within the sphere of experimental investigation. All creative scientists know that the true laboratory is the mind, where behind illusions they uncover the laws of truth. The lectures will announce new discoveries, demonstrated for the first time in these halls. Through regular publication of the work of the Bose Institute, these Indian contributions will reach the world.

It was the wish of Bose that the facilities of this Institute be available, so far as possible, to workers from all countries. As far back as twenty-five centuries India has welcomed to its ancient universities at Nalanda and Taxila, scholars from all parts of the world.

Nonfiction

THIRTY-SEVEN

George Washington Carver's Accomplishments

Moses and Susan Carver adopted George Washington Carver after his parents passed away. As George grew up with the Carvers he learned to cook, sew and do the laundry. As George drew and embroidered Aunt Susan saw his artistic talent.

George Washington Carver was smart. He learned to read a blue bound copy of Webster's Elementary spelling Book. He asked a lot of questions about many things. George enjoyed listening to Moses Carver play the fiddle. George loved working in the garden. He wanted to know about everything that lived there such as animals, vegetables and minerals as well as the tallest corn to the potato bugs.

George began experimenting on his own, trying to find out what sort of soil suited each flower and vegetable. Young George was known to have a green thumb. He was called the plant doctor. George worked in the woods and came home with rocks, minerals and all sorts of plants and creatures. His foster parents observed that he was a special, curious child. Aunt Susan made George empty his pockets out in the yard. She didn't want crawling, flying, hopping or slithering.

George wanted to know every strange stone, flower, insect, bird or beast. He had no one to teach him. Looking back, he said it was as if "his very soul was thirsty for an education." Moses and Susan Carver hired a young educated fellow from Missouri to give George and his brother some lessons. George asked a lot of questions and more than the tutor had answers. At the age of 12 George walked eight miles to attend school in the town of Neosho to receive an education. George never lived with the Carvers again.

Between 1877 and 1890 George Washington Carver made loyal friends and he worked hard. He was a poor, brilliant black teenager. He had to earn his own way in the world. Discouraging, even terrifying incidents littered his path to becoming an educated man.

In Neosho, Missouri, George met Andrew and Mariah Watkins, a childless black couple who offered him a home in return for help with the chores. Aunt Mariah was wise in the ways of medicinal plants. She helped women bring their babies into the world. George helped her with the laundry. He came to admire Mrs. Watkins.

Mr. Frost was confronted with George, who was an intense, skinny, country boy with shabby clothes, and an oddly high-pitched voice. He was eager to learn and he asked many questions. George made the best of his opportunities. He studied and dug deeply into what books were available. He washed clothes with washtubs. He went to the African Methodist Episcopal Church with Aunt Mariah. His character was very much shaped by that of his industrial very religious landlady.

When George was thirteen he moved to Kansas in the 1870s. George learned about sodbusters, black and white and what they discovered. George sent word to Moses and Susan Carver that he had found work and a place to live in Fort Scott, Kansas.

Reconstruction was a complex painful era after the Civil War. Freedom wasn't true freedom. Some 40,000 black troops had lost their lives in the Civil War, mostly as Union soldiers fighting for their freedom. The U.S.A. was faced with nearly four million freed folks, many of whom were broken, homeless and suffering from a lack of schooling and medical care. In 1865, the American Congress set up an agency known as the Freedmen's Bureau to help.

More than 4,300 schools were founded and at first idealistic white folks signed up to teach newly freed blacks. Budgets tightened. Some schools grew shabby, understaffed, fewer and farther between. Still, there were those that blossomed into outstanding black educational institutions, such as Fisk University in Nashville, Tennessee; Howard University in the nation's capital and Virginia's Hampton Institute (now Hampton University). Booker T. Washington was a student and teacher there.

George Washington Carver observed severe injustice against black people. He witnessed lynching and other cruel behavior towards blacks. However, George continued to gather local flora and fauna. Years later he explained his point of view: "More and more as we come closer and closer in touch with nature and its teachings we are able to see the Divine."

It was during these years that George went back to Diamond to visit the Carvers. George added typing as another skill and he got a job in Missouri as an office clerk in the Kansas City train station. George applied at the Highland College. The President of this college found out that George Washington Carver was colored. He turned George down even after George spent money to enroll at Highland College. As a result, George was discouraged and he didn't go to college. Now it was back to the washtubs or whatever work he could find.

A year later George Washington Carver became a homesteader. He bought a quarter section (half a mile square or 160 acres) in 1886. He borrowed equipment to plant corn, a garden and trees. He dug wells. However, he didn't find enough water. When George wasn't busy over his crops, vegetables and washtubs or caring for his chickens he made music for his friends. He attended church on Sundays.

In 1887 George completed a little sod house on the prairie. It was 14 feet square. The walls were thick, making the indoors cool in summer and warm in winter. George Carver was about 23 years old when he experienced a blizzard in 1888. George moved to Iowa when the 1880s came to an end.

Life was bitter for George Carver in Winterset, Iowa. George met the Milhollands who were impressed with his sweet singing voice and his deep spiritual nature, his intelligence and talents. In time, they encouraged him to try again to get into college. So, George enrolled at Simpson College in Indianola, Iowa. With his tubs, boiler and washboard, he would still have to earn a living. He was receiving an education as well as acceptance. He wrote that his fellow students "made him believe I was a real human being."

George studied English composition and grammar, arithmetic, singing and piano. He excelled in drawing. He was very good at painting flowers. In his spare time George experimented with plants, creating hybrids by cross-fertilizing (combining cells) from different kinds of vegetables, flowers or fruit trees to create a new variety. He would graft (attach) a scion (a bud or cutting) from one plant to another so they would grow together. Grafting is a way to propagate (reproduce) seedless plants or to improve the quality of an existing plant.

In 1891, George Washington Carver was the first and only black student to attend Iowa State College of Agriculture and Mechanical Arts in the town of Ames, about 30 miles north of the state capital at Des Moines. At first, George had to endure some name-calling and being ordered to eat his dormitory meals in the basement with the servants. George studied, went to church, and struggled to survive on what he could earn. He refused to take money from anyone unless he had earned it. George continued to draw and sketch and he took notes in class.

George wore homemade clothes. He gathered wild berries, dandelion greens, wild onions and mushrooms to eat. In the five years green thumb George spent at Ames, he excelled in botany (the science of plants) and horticulture (the science and art of growing fruits, flowers, vegetables and ornamental plants). George Washington Carver's most influential professor, Dr. Louis H. Pammel, was a mycologist, one who studies fungi such as mushrooms, mildews, molds and lichens. They feed off plants, animals or rotting matter. Unlike other plants, a fungus has no chlorophyll (the substance that enables green plants to take energy from sunlight). Fungi do better in the dark. Some are harmful, causing Dutch elm disease or athlete's foot.

Before George Washington Carver finished college, he collected more than a thousand fungus specimens. He became an expert researcher. His genuine warmth and enthusiasm as well as his abilities helped most people to overcome their negative attitude about Negroes or "colored", as African Americans were commonly known back then. George was active in church and YMCA (Young Men's Christian Association) activities as well as clubs on campus. He drilled with the college's military unit. George performed in plays and recited poems and participated in music.

George Washington Carver received his Bachelor of Science in 1894. He was the first black person to graduate from Iowa State University. He worked toward his Masters degree for two years. He worked on scientific papers and he studied fungi. He conducted horticultural experiments in the college's greenhouse, of which he was now in charge. He was the first black instructor at Iowa State University. They soon discovered that Assistant Botany Professor Carver had a natural gift for teaching.

George accepted an offer from Booker T. Washington, the best-known black man in America, after Frederick Douglas had passed away in 1895. George Washington Carver looked forward to teaching at Tuskegee, Alabama in 1896. It would be his home for the next 47 years. Coming to Tuskegee would fulfill "the one ideal of my life to be of the greatest good to the greatest number of my people possible and to this end I have been preparing myself for these many years."

Booker T. Washington established the Institute on July 4, 1881 with 30 students known as the Tuskegee Normal and Industrial Institute in a leaky wreck of a church in rural Alabama. "The goal of this school and other such schools was teaching useful trades to newly freed slaves, equipping them to go out into the world and teach others to free themselves with hard work and education," stated Cheryl Harness.

George Washington Carver felt that his talents were God-given and that he was God-chosen to teach is people how to restore their beaten down selves. He felt like a missionary, excited and humble. George Washington Carver accomplished the following things. His theory that plants and animals evolved over eons from a few shared ancestors caused people to rethink the nature of life on Earth, including their own. This "census-taker of the sky" recorded and classified stars. He proved that the heavens were an expanding universe of galaxies. This black, American chemist devised sight-saving and pain-relieving medicines. He proved how diseases and germs were linked, then developed ways to fight them. He made the life-saving discovery of germ-killing penicillin. He found out how genes are arranged in our cells' chromosomes. He pioneered genetics (the science of heredity). Time, space, gravity, matter and energy—the 20th century's best known sciences revolutionized peoples' thinking about these concepts. This biologist advanced our knowledge of the cell. He also discovered over one hundred products made from sweet potatoes and peanuts. He was born in 1865 and passed away in 1943 at the age of 78.

Professor George Washington Carver's cardinal virtues were as follows. (1) Be clean both inside and outside, (2) Who neither looks up to the rich or down to the poor, (3) Who loses, if need be, without squealing, (4) Who wins without bragging, (5) Who is always considerate of women, children and old people, (6) Who is brave to lie, (7) Who is too generous to cheat, (8) Who takes his share of the world and lets other people have theirs.

Nonfiction

THIRTY-EIGHT

Swans Are Graceful

Swans are considered to be one of the most graceful and beautiful birds in the world. They tend to flock together in ponds, lagoons and lakes. Flamingos are beautiful, colorful birds. However, swans are more graceful and docile.

Observing swans is a miraculous experience because their calm, peaceful and graceful movements cause observers to admire how they move in the water. Artists have painted scenes of floating swans in lakes and ponds.

Swans have majestic white wings and many feathers. They balance their bodies as they glide their feet in the water. Swans follow a leader swan across lakes, ponds and streams. They are fascinating to watch. Swan Lake Ballet is famous. Ballerinas gracefully move on a large stage in ballerina outfits and ballet shoes in groups.

Nonfiction

THIRTY-NINE

Identical Twins

Identical twins look exactly alike. They have the same hair coloring and eye color. They grow in similar stages. Generally, identical twins grow up together and experience step-by-step stages.

Identical twins have identical DNA. Identical twins may be two girls or two boys. While they grow up together they may develop the same habits. They may be similar in personality characteristics.

However, though identical twins may look exactly alike they may develop different interests, hobbies and they may think differently. Personality difference may distinguish identical twins. For instance, one identical twin may have different thoughts and opinions about people, places and issues. Each identical twin has his or her individual and personal thoughts and consciousness. Identical twins may react differently to situations and experiences.

Identical twins may not pass away at the same time. One twin may outlive the other twin. Each of them may dress differently and wear a different hairstyle. One identical twin may gain more weight. One twin may look older or younger than the other identical twin. Each identical twin may have a slightly different voice quality.

So, identical twins have specific differences even though they look alike. They need to find their own personal identity. Even if they grow up together they have an opportunity to develop their own personalities and talents. They should learn to become independent and self sufficient. Identical twins are recognized for their different personalities.

Cecelia Frances Page

Nonfiction

FORTY

Old Fashioned Cooking

Old fashioned cooking is when food is cooked from scratch. Meat is roasted in roasting pans. Meat is grilled or fried. Vegetables are prepared from scratch. Vegetables are washed out and steamed in sauce pans. Fruit is cut and eaten raw or cooked.

Original, homemade sauces and gravies are made from scratch. All the ingredients are mixed together first. Then the ingredients are stirred in a sauce pan until cooked. Sauces and gravy are poured over meat and potatoes.

Casserole dishes are prepared from recipes. Scalloped potatoes with cheese and creamy sauce can be prepared. Spaghetti with meatballs with spaghetti sauce is delicious. Zucchini and squash can be prepared in a casserole dish. Lasagna prepared with pasta, meat and tomato sauce can be prepared from scratch. Noodle dishes with tuna or hamburger is another casserole dish. Homemade sauce should be added to the noodles dish.

Homemade pies, cakes, cookies and muffins are prepared with specific ingredients and baked in the oven. Pudding is prepared with special ingredients from scratch.

Many people eat food in microwave ovens. However, this type of heat destroys the food value. Old fashioned ovens are better to bake food. TV dinners, frozen packaged food and canned food have replaced old fashion cooking. Yet, old fashion cooking is a healthier way to prepare food. Use organic vegetables and fruits. Also, select naturally grown wheat, barley, beans, rice and potatoes which have not been sprayed with man-made insecticides. Healthy organic foods which are not overcooked are best to prepare. Eating healthy foods keeps us healthier.

Fiction

FORTY-ONE

The China Tea Set

Anna Sullivan was a collector of tea cups, saucers, delicate wine and champagne glasses and beautiful plates and silverware. She displayed her collection of finery in shelves and glass-covered cabinets. Anna kept collecting more and more finery.

One day Anna went to Chinatown in New York City. She walked from shop to shop to look for a China tea set because this was something she wanted and didn't have in her collection. Finally, after browsing in a number of shops, Anna came to a shop which had a variety of China tea sets. She carefully looked at each China tea set. Beautiful, artistic and nature designs were painted on the teapots and small tea cups.

Each China tea set was unique and special to observe. Anna liked all of the tea sets. She had difficulty in deciding which tea set to select. The price for each tea set varied. After looking over the tea sets for fifteen minutes she finally selected a golden tea pot with turquoise, intricate designs with six matching tea cups. She paid the storekeeper $20 for this tea set.

The storekeeper wrapped the elegant tea set in a box with soft, white paper which was covered over the tea pot. Each cup was individually wrapped and put in the box. Anna took the box with the tea set and walked out of the shop in Chinatown. She decided to go home. It was getting dark. Blinking lights were turned on to add light and color.

Anna went on the streetcar back to the street where she lived. She saw blinking lights along the way home. She stepped off the streetcar near her apartment. She walked up a long staircase to enter the six story apartment and unlocked the front door. She walked in with her package. She laid the package on the dining room table. Anna unwrapped the teapot and six tea cups. She placed this magnificent China tea set in an open shelf so it could be displayed in the dining room. This China tea set stood out and was more beautiful than the rest of Anna's collection.

A week later, Anna invited five friends to her home to serve tea and refreshments. She had an opportunity to use her new China tea set. She prepared a delicious tea pot of Jasmine hot tea. When the tea was ready she poured tea in the six tea cups around the dining room table. She had already placed Chinese cookies, crackers and cut fruit for her guest to enjoy.

Anna sat down to join her friends who were Jane, Susan, Pamela, Tina and Marlene. She met her friends at school and church. Anna was glad to have this tea party. Her friends admired the new China tea set. They made comments about how beautiful the tea pot and tea cups were. This was a special occasion.

Anna's friends decided to go to Chinatown in New York City to purchase their own China tea sets because they were so impressed with Anna's tea set.

Nonfiction

FORTY-TWO

Churchgoers

Churchgoers tend to be more religious as a rule. They attend Church regularly to worship God and Jesus Christ, Buddha, Mother Mary, the Divine Director and certain gods and goddesses.

Churchgoers attend church to participate in communion, prayers, sharing water, bread and singing religious songs. They may kneel to worship. They pray fervently to become close to God and Masters. Church is a place to lift one's vibrations. It is a special place to share activities such as potlucks, picnics, sewing bees, religious plays, singing, games and parties.

Churchgoers meet other people who attend church. They can make new friends at church. There are receptions, funerals and special programs at church.

There are many churches to select from and to attend. Each church has different ministers, priests and leaders. Each church has different speakers and messages. Different songs are sung. Music presentations are unique and performed at different times.

Churchgoers usually are active in communities. They have a more interesting way of living because of their religious fervor. They usually are more adjusted and are happier because they feel close to God. They may be better citizens because they believe in peace and brotherhood.

Fiction

FORTY-THREE

The Shopkeeper

Ernestina Gates owned a boutique shop in San Francisco, California entitled Ernestina's Boutique Shop. She bought this shop fifteen years ago. She had arranged many shelves and tables with glass frames. Ernestina had bought many unique items to place in her boutique shop such as unusual dresses, jackets, coats, purses, scarves, knitted sweaters, jewelry, stockings, pants, blouses, men's suits, formal gowns, ties and a variety of glassware.

The boutique shop looked colorful, exotic and was well arranged so customers could locate items easily. Ernestina had been a shopkeeper for twenty years. She was experienced in how to deal with customers. She had developed a reputation of having quality selections plus reasonable prices in her boutique shop.

Many customers came to the boutique shop to browse around. Many bought items here. Ernestina was a successful shopkeeper. She often showed people around her shop. She kept her boutique shop clean and very attractive. Customers would come back to purchase more items because they appreciated the quality merchandise at Ernestina's Boutique Shop.

Customers came from near and far to select items at Ernestina's Boutique Shop. Ernestina packaged their items in attractive boxes and shopping bags. Customers were impressed with the way she packaged their purchased items. Ernestina continued to do well for many years.

Then, a Great Depression came one year. People were broke. Many customers stopped coming downtown San Francisco to shop. Ernestina's business slowed down. Fortunately, she owned her shop. So, she didn't have to pay rent. However, she still had to pay annual taxes for her shop and business income. It was a difficult time for Ernestina and many other shopkeepers. She managed to pay her annual taxes. Her annual income was much less than proceeding years. Somehow, she managed to get by.

Several years went by, and Ernestina managed to keep her boutique shop open. She continued to purchase exotic items to put into her shop. Business began to pick up after five years. Finally, when Ernestina was 67 years old she decided to retire. She sold her boutique shop to an eager couple who wanted to purchase it.

Ernestina took the money she was paid for the boutique shop and invested in annuities. She also received a Social Security payment once a month. She received $900 a month because she had invested in Social Security every year for many years. She received interest every month from four annuities. She received $2,100 a month for interest money. So, Ernestina received $3,000 a month to live on. She lived in an apartment which had two bedrooms which was paid off over 30 years.

Ernestina was free to do what she wanted to do after she retired. She saved over $550,000 plus she had invested another $450,000 into the four annuities. Ernestina decided to travel around the world. She began by taking several cruises to exotic locations such as Mexico, the Bahamas Islands, Tahiti, Europe and around South America. She met interesting people on her travels. She enjoyed delicious cuisine and gourmet food on her journeys around the world. She saw many scenic views and locations. She especially enjoyed sunrises and sunsets.

Ernestina had never married because she was busy running the boutique shop for many years. She took photographs on her trips abroad. She was happy because she enjoyed traveling many exciting, adventuresome places in the world.

Fiction

FORTY-FOUR

Brad's Conflicts

Brad Mallory was attending high school in Alameda County in California. He was handicapped so he sat in a wheelchair because his legs were lame. Brad felt self conscious about his handicapped condition.

In different classrooms he sat in a wheelchair along one side of the room. He was the only one who was sitting in a wheel chair. He resented having to sit n a wheelchair because he had been very athletic at one time. His life had changed considerably after his accident when he went surfing one day and crashed which paralyzed his legs.

Brad thought his classmates were gossiping about his handicap behind his back. He felt insecure and helpless. He felt inferior because he was unable to do the physical activities his peers could do such as walk, run, hike, jog and do standing exercises.

Brad was lifted into a swimming pool to exercise. He was able to hold onto the edge of the pool so he could move his legs in the water. Brad was able to exercise regularly so he could regain strength in his body.

Day by day, month by month Brad became stronger physically. He was determined to walk again and to experience a normal life.

He went to a Physical Therapist who helped him exercise properly. Eventually, Brad regained strength in his legs.

Finally, after a year, Brad was able to walk with crutches and then a cane. He was able to walk in time without crutches and a cane. He took walks up and down the street where he lived to continue to become stronger. Brad no longer sat in a wheelchair at school. He was able to sit in a regular desk in his high school classrooms.

Brad began to regain his self confidence. He had overcome his physical handicap. He felt better about himself. He didn't think his classmates were gossiping about him anymore. He was more cheerful and began to overcome his conflicts. He had learned to overcome his fear and depression about his previous handicaps. Brad was grateful to experience a normal life again. He even went dancing again. He was able to join in sports such as volleyball, tennis and baseball.

Brad was able to date high school girls again because he could now drive a car. He realized that he could fulfill his wishes as long as he pursued his goals. He was able to fulfill his goals. He was a much happier person.

Fiction

FORTY-FIVE

Tale of Bliss

Miranda was a young lady with a light spirit. She pranced into the forest in her domain. She radiated with light and a magical presence. Miranda floated around the magical forest. She had twinkling wings which sparkled as she flew around.

Miranda continued to fly much deeper into the forest. She greeted blue jays, owls, foxes, rabbits, and other creatures with a cheerful tone in her voice as she cheerfully said hello. The creatures of the forest adored Miranda. They looked forward to seeing her fly through the forest.

As Miranda continued her journey she came to the other side of the forest. She flew into a big, colorful canyon. She saw hillsides in the distance. Colorful red and orange canyon rocks appeared on either side of the canyon. Miranda flew up close to a canyon ledge. She saw baby hawks in nests on the ledge.

Miranda decided to fly to the ledge where the baby hawks were nesting. They appeared hungry and helpless. Their baby feather fluff was coming out. They opened their beaks to receive food. Of course, Miranda didn't have any food to give them. She realized they were very hungry. She wondered where their mother hawk was.

Miranda stood on the ledge for some time to observe the three baby hawks. They moved around in their nest and made baby hawk sounds. Miranda tried not to frighten the baby hawks. She began to sing to them. The baby hawks listened to Miranda's sweet voice. They appeared calmer. Miranda waited for many hours. The mother hawk never appeared to feed her babies.

Miranda decided to go look for the mother hawk. She flew around the canyon and over a flowing stream. She traveled for many miles looking for the mother hawk. She was unable to find it. So, she decided to go back into the canyon. She carefully looked for the ledge where the baby hawks were nesting. It began to rain. Raindrops came down in torrents. Miranda ignored the rain even if she became sopping wet. She was concerned about the baby hawks because they were helpless still and they depended on their mother to feed them.

Miranda knew that the baby hawks would starve to death unless they were fed. She located their nest. She noticed they were still hungry and they were cold from the rain. Miranda decided that she would look after these three baby hawks. So, she carried the baby hawks in a cloth bag over her shoulder. Then she flew out of the canyon with the hawks until she reached a place miles away where she dwelled in the forest.

Miranda created a new nest in a tree on a large branch. She placed the three baby hawks in the new nest. She fed each of them pieces of meat. They swallowed down the meat quickly. Miranda continued to look after the three hawks until they grew up. They had to learn to fly. Miranda flew in the sky with them to guide them so they could learn to use their wings and to keep their balance while they learned to fly around in the forest, the valleys nearby and even to the ocean near the coast. She enjoyed the warm sunshine, the pristine beaches as well as the verdant-green forests. She smelled the pleasant fragrance of pine needles and bark. She observed vivid sunrises and spectacular sunsets. She enjoyed flying around to experience nature. She glittered in the sunlight and she sang blissful songs to the flowers, trees and creatures around her.

FORTY-SIX

Inner Dimension Contacts

There are inner dimensions which are invisible to the physical eyes. These invisible dimensions are very beautiful. Sparkling light blazes in these inner planes. Angels fly around and there are pillars with different colors and sizes.

Spirit beings float around in inner dimensions. Heavenly designs exist everywhere in these inner spheres. Heavenly hosts sing beautiful, harmonic, celestial songs. Inner, higher dimensions glow with rainbow colors and rays of light.

Masters dwell in higher, inner dimensions to serve. They practice the Golden Rule and Brotherhood. Masters exist in immortal forms. They emanate light and send out a higher vibration with eternal love.

The physical body does not exist in the inner dimensions. Physical forms exist in the outer dimension in the world. The astral plane is parallel within the invisible dimension. The astral plane is a finer image and reflection of the physical plane.

The sun is radiant and blazes in other planes. Circles of light expand outward and interiorly reflecting pastel colors. The inner eye is used to look at the inner dimensions.

Dancing spirits glide around and fly with their wings of light moving in and out within inner dimensions. Astral beings witness cosmic images and have their spirit blueprint recorded on the higher, inner dimensions by the Divine Creator. Each soul is contacted by angels, archangels, elohim and Masters interiorly to help to promote soul protection and growth. We are not alone because we can be guided by higher, celestial beings. There are seven planes of consciousness and seven color rays which exist in God's creation. We need to learn to become aware of matter, force and consciousness on different planes.

Nonfiction

FORTY-SEVEN

About Banks and Bankers

Banks have been established so people can place their money into savings and checking accounts. Customers of banks can apply for home loans, business loans and miscellaneous loans. Living trust funds can be created for customers who want to leave their estate funds to loved ones and charities.

Customers come to their bank regularly to deposit money into their savings and checking accounts. They earn interest money on their money kept in savings and checking accounts. Many customers obtain special deposit boxes to place money certificates, wills, life insurance policies, etc,

Banks are kept open because people make investments, take out loans and have notary republic work done as well as take out home loans. Banks depend on investments to keep them financially feasible and available to the public. There are many banks around the world such as Bank of America, Bank of England, International Bank, commercial banks, county banks, Citibank, Wells Fargo Bank and state banks. Swiss banks keep large, private deposits for very wealthy people.

Bankers are administrators, business transactors, tellers, notary republics, clerks, bookkeepers and accountants. Bankers must be accurate when exchanging money, depositing and withdrawing

Cecelia Frances Page

money. They must know how to use computers, adding machines and calculators. They are required to be able to look up customer accounts and keep computer and written customer records.

Certain bankers need to know how to interview people who are applying for home and business loans. They must investigate whether applicants are qualified to receive loans. Bankers must investigate phony checks from scammers. Banks can go bankrupt because phony checks are cashed for very large amounts. People who do not pay off their loans from banks cause banks to lose a lot of money.

American bank bonds are available at most American banks. Some bonds have been known to lose value. Customers applying for bonds may be taking a risk. Bonds must mature before they can be cashed. Cashier checks and money orders are used by many people. They must be shown how to fill out cashier checks and money orders.

Bankers should have some bank training and business sense to maintain efficient banking and successful bank negotiations. Big bankers need to develop sound and effective bank policies. The public depend on effective, reliable banks and banking methods. People in the world depend on banks to promote finances and financial security. Bankers should not misuse money at banks. They should protect large sums of money.

Nonfiction

FORTY-EIGHT

A New World Economy

A new world economy may be needed soon. Many people in the world are unemployed. Approximately on a world scale 30% of all world people may be jobless. This means jobless people are not able to meet their financial needs. They must receive food at food banks and at church charity lunches which are usually only once a day. Jobless people may be homeless as well. They must sleep in alleys, streets, under trees and on the ground. They literally must camp outdoors.

During the daytime, homeless people generally walk around carrying backpacks and they are pushing go-carts around. Homeless people depend on others to donate money so they can buy food. Homeless individuals move around to find ways to survive.

If there was a stable world economy more people would be employed. They would be able to pay their bills such as food and shelter and miscellaneous items. There would be far less hunger and homeless conditions. People would be more prosperous. They would be healthier and happier.

How can a stable world economy be established in the world? It will take careful world planning to establish a successful world economy. Natural resources must be distributed properly around the world in every country. Individuals need to bring about a stable economy everywhere. A new world currency should be developed to meet the needs of the down and out.

A new world currency should be distributed in each country. Goods and services should be given to each country according to their needs. Jobs should be provided to everyone. The homeless should be given homes with proper shelter to protect them. Food should be distributed to everyone. Money should not become an obstacle. Everyone should be able to survive by having enough food and shelter.

A world government based on the Golden Rule and brotherhood where all humanity on Earth work for the common good and welfare of everyone will protect humanity around the world. Survival of human beings can take place if humanity focuses on the welfare of all life and survival of humanity. We should avoid war, personal greed and focus on all countries as being important and deserving to thrive and do well. World currency should be given to all the world's people. Inflation should be avoided so money will maintain its value.

Poverty, disease and starvation should be overcome. There is no need for poverty. Disease can be prevented. Starvation should be stopped if all humanity is provided with enough food. A world government focused on meeting the basic needs of all humanity is the best way to protect all humanity. The goal should be to provide safety, abundance and a better way of life in the world. The goal should be to maintain balance, equilibrium and love for one another and be willing to serve one another.

Fiction

FORTY-NINE

Experience at a Pub

Pam and Jerry Whitman went to the corner pub as often as they could to unwind after work hours. They were glad the pubs were in their neighborhood in the city of Detroit, Michigan. They walked to the closest pub to relax and have some beer.

When Pam and Jerry entered the nearby pub they heard background music. Jazz was heard from a stereo system. Several people were sitting at a bar. Several couples were sitting at tables. All of them were drinking an alcoholic beverage. They were listening to the music.

Pam and Jerry sat at a table. A bartender walked over to their table and asked them what they wanted to order. Pam ordered a nonalcoholic O'Doulls. Jerry ordered a Bud Light. The bartender went back to the bar to get the two beers.

Meanwhile, Pam and Jerry looked around the pub. The jazz music suddenly stopped. Karoke music was played with the words on a television screen so people could follow along and sing the words as they read each line on the television. Pam and Jerry began singing along with other people at the bar. They sang several songs.

The bartender came back to Pam and Jerry's table with two beers. The bartender placed two ice-cold large glass cups on the table near Pam and Jerry. Pam and Jerry poured their beer into their large glass cups. They began drinking their beer.

Karoke music was still being played. People in the bar continued to sing along as they read the words off of the television screen. Cocktail waiters brought peanuts to the tables as well as crackers. Pam and Jerry munched some peanuts and crackers. They sipped their cold beer. Then they continued to sing karoke songs.

Pam and Jerry spent an hour at the pub. Several more people came into the pub. They sat near Pam and Jerry at nearby tables. They joined in with the karoke music after they ordered drinks. One couple who were sitting close to Pam and Jerry decided to talk to them. Cara spoke to Pam. She said, "Hi. I remember seeing you here several nights ago. Do you come here often?" Pam replied, "I like to come to this pub. My husband and I come here often to unwind." Cara responded, "This is my third time at this pub. I like to unwind, too!"

Jerry was listening. He was sipping a third cold beer. He noticed Cara's companion. Jerry said, "Hi. I am Jerry. Who are you?" Phil replied, "I am Phil. My wife and I have been going to different pubs. We decided to come here tonight. We may be going to London soon. There are a variety of pubs there. Have you been to London?" Phil answered, "No. I haven't been to London. I would like to go there. I hear London is a wonderful place for Ale!" Phil smiled and responded, "My wife and I have traveled to Europe several times. We plan to take another trip there soon." The men continued to visit for awhile.

Pam reached out to Cara. She said, "I like to go ice skating. My husband and I have been skating for years. Do you know how to ice skate?" Cara answered, "No. I have never learned to ice skate. I like to play tennis. I play tennis regularly. Tennis is a lot of fun to play. I find tennis to be challenging as well. Where do you go ice skating?" Cara replied, "There is an ice rink down in the Arena. It has been open to the public for years. I go there at least once a week to ice skate."

Pam and Jerry became acquainted with Cara and Phil. Before they left the pub they changed telephone numbers so they could keep in touch by phone. Pam and Jerry left the pub at 10:20 p.m. to go home. They would have to get up early the next morning to go to work again. It would be Thursday. They looked forward to going to this pub again soon to unwind. They enjoyed meeting people here as well as participating with singing Karoke music. They could relax and could drink beer as well.

Fiction

FIFTY

Important Moments

Important moments occur in our lives. Sometimes important moments are sudden and even unexpected. Such experiences as enjoying a birthday celebration, dating someone special, receiving a worthwhile job during an interview as well as getting married are important moments in one's life.

Rosanne Harrison had important moments which occurred in her life. When she was five years old she remembered her first day of school. She was afraid to go to kindergarten. Her mother took Rosanne to the school bus which stopped down the street from her home. Rosanne's mother took Rosanne to the school bus which stopped down the street from her home. Rosanne's mother put her on the bus. Rosanne sat down near the front of the bus near the bus driver. He drove the bus to a neighborhood elementary school.

Rosanne got off the school bus and walked into the main school building. She needed to be shown to her classroom. Someone in the school office took Rosanne to Room 10 to Mrs. Foster's kindergarten. Mrs. Foster was busy with other new students when Rosanne stood inside the doorway. She waited there because she didn't know what to do.

Finally, Mrs. Foster asked all the children to sit down at a desk. So, everyone selected a desk facing the teacher who stood in front of the classroom. Rosanne sat near the front of the classroom. She wondered what kindergarten would be like. She felt nervous. She had never been away from home without her parents. She would have to adjust to school.

Rosanne missed her mother. She wanted to go home. She began to cry suddenly. Mrs. Foster noticed Rosanne sobbing. She went over to comfort Rosanne. Mrs. Foster looked at Rosanne warmly. She smiled at Rosanne and said, "Hello. Don't cry. You will enjoy school." Mrs. Foster continued to look at Rosanne with understanding. She had been teaching kindergarten for many years. The first day of school was usually traumatic for some kindergarteners who had never been away from home and from their parents.

Rosanne remembered how nice and warm Mrs. Foster was to her especially on her first day of school. Rosanne was able to adjust better to school. She learned to fingerpaint, print and say the ABCs. She learned to print her name and to count. She participated in singing and playing games. Rosanne enjoyed kindergarten. She had experienced many important moments and experiences at school.

Another important time was when Roxanne went to college. She didn't know what to major in. She hadn't selected a career. One day a mutual friend suggested that Rosanne go to the college library to the reference desk to request some careers. She read about duties, responsibilities, working conditions, annual salaries and hours of employment.

Rosanne's friend told her to select a career based on her abilities, interests and capabilities. Rosanne had developed a variety of interests and hobbies. After studying the career books, Rosanne decided to select teaching elementary school. She liked to work with children. She could play the piano and sing. She was interested in teaching Reading, Arithmetic, English, Spelling, Art and P.E. as well as Social Studies and Science.

This was a very important time for Rosanne when she was selecting a career and a major to study in college. Her life was changed by her career as an elementary school teacher. She pursued her B.A. in Education and a minor in Music.

When Rosanne went for job interviews after she graduated from college she experienced important moments at interviews. She recalled an important interview in Santa Maria, California. She was interviewed by a lady in the Personnel Department. She was asked many questions such as: "Why do you want to work here in Santa Maria School District? What objectives and purposes will you use while teaching? What discipline methods will you use? Why did you become a teacher? Are you willing to participate in school activities beyond your classroom responsibilities?" Rosanne carefully answered these questions. She was dressed in a beautiful dress with an attractive hair style. The interviewer seemed impressed with Roxanne's answers. Rosanne had submitted her resume during the interview.

The personnel director who interviewed Rosanne said she would contact Rosanne in a few days to let her know what her decision would be about the teaching position. Rosanne went home and waited to hear from the personnel director. She hoped to receive this teaching position. She hadn't received any other teaching positions yet.

In a few days Rosanne received a call from the Personnel Department. She was told that she had been accepted to teach Grade Six. She would start after Labor Day in September of that same year. Rosanne was overjoyed. This was a very important moment in her life. She would be starting her first year of teaching when summer was over.

Another important moment was when Rosanne met a man who would eventually propose to her. She dated Ryan Collier for approximately one year. One day Ryan took Rosanne to a beautiful waterfall at a National Park. He asked Roxanne to marry him in this romantic setting. Rosanne accepted his marriage proposal immediately. She was very much in love with Ryan, who she felt was charming, debonair and handsome. She felt genuinely in love with him. She knew she would be happy with him.

Rosanne reflected back on other important moments in her life. She recalled important decisions that she had made through the years. She had lived a creative, productive life.

Nonfiction

FIFTY-ONE

An Experience in Cosmic Consciousness

Paramahansa Yogananda described Cosmic Consciousness as "An oceanic joy broke upon calm endless shores of my soul. The Spirit of God, I realized, is exhaustless bliss. His body is countless tissues of light. A swelling glory within me began to envelope towns, continents, the earth, solar and stellar systems, tenuous nebulae, and floating universes. The entire cosmos, gently luminous like a city seen afar at night, glimmered within the infinitude of my being. The dazzling light beyond the sharply etched global outlines faded slightly at the farthest edges. There I saw a mellow radiance, ever undiminished. It was indescribably subtle. The planetary pictures were formed of a grosser light."

Yogananda continued to describe the Cosmos. He stated, "The divine dispersion of rays poured from an Eternal Source, blazing into galaxies, transfigured with ineffable auras. Again and again I saw the creative beams condense into constellations; then resolve into sheets of transparent flame. By rhythmic reversion, sextillion worlds passed into diaphanous luster; then fire became firmament."

Yogananda, who was enlightened, continued to describe his experience with cosmic consciousness. He expressed, "I cognize the center of the empyrean as a point of intuitive perception in my heart.

Irradiating splendor issued from my nucleus to every part of the universal structure. Blissful "amrita," nectar of immortality, pulsated through me with a quicksilver-like fluidity. The creative voice of God I heard resounding as AUM, the vibration of the Cosmic Motor."

Yogananda went on to describe his cosmic experiences. He said, "It is the Spirit of God that actively sustains every form and force in the Universe. Yet, he is transcendental and aloof in the blissful, uncreated void beyond the worlds of vibratory phenomena." Master Yogananda explained, "Those who attain self-realization on Earth live a similar twofold existence. Conscientiously performing their work in the world, they are yet immersed in an inward beatitude."

Yogananda said, "The Lord has created all men from the illimitable joy of His being. Though they are painfully cramped by the body, God nevertheless expects that men made in His image shall ultimately rise above all sense, identifications and reunite with Him." He continued to state, "The cosmic vision left many permanent lessons. By daily stilling my thoughts, I could win release from the delusive conviction that my body was a mass of flesh and bones traversing the hard sail of matter. The breath and the restless mind, I saw, are like storms that lash the ocean of light into waves of material forms---earth, sky, human beings, animals, birds, trees. No perception of the infinite as One Light can be had except by calming those storms. As often as I quieted the two nature tumults, I beheld the multitudinous waves of the ocean, when a tempest subsides, serenely dissolved into unity."

Yogananda said, "A master bestows the divine experience of Cosmic Consciousness when his disciple, by meditation, has strengthened his mind to a degree where the vast vistas would not overwhelm him. Mere intellectual willingness or open-mindedness is not enough. Only adequate enlargement of consciousness by yoga practice and devotional bhakti can prepare one to absorb the liberating shock of omnipresence. The divine experience comes with a natural inevitability to the sincere devotee. His intense craving begins to pull at God with an irresistible force. The Lord as the Cosmic Vision is drawn by that magnetic order into the seeker's range of consciousness."

For more details on Yogananda's great, inspirational, spiritual teachings, be sure to read his landmark book AUTOBIOGRAPHY OF A YOGI, and refer to the Self Realization Fellowship he established.

Nonfiction

FIFTY-TWO

The Mystery of Crop Circles

In 2009 dozens of new crop circles appeared in Britain. Many crop circles appear to be more complex each year. There are many theories about what causes these formations. Some people believe crop circles are caused by light beings from other dimensions. Others conjecture crop circles are caused by devas, elemental spirits, angels, elves, leprechauns or other legendary beings. A popular theory for these formations is extraterrestrials in hovering UFOs. Of course, many skeptics believe all crop circles are made by pranksters as hoaxes.

However, the formations made by confessed hoaxers are far too simple and small to account for many other complex crop circles. These pranksters used wood planks and common tools that are easy to trace. The much larger and more perplexing crop circles caused molecular and structural changes in the stalks that the pranksters found impossible to duplicate. Fifty pranksters required two days to create a very simple design. Complex designs appeared in less than an hour.

Furthermore, there have been numerous sightings of large UFOs and small, glowing orbs flying around crop circles. There have been multiple witnesses to some of these sightings.

In 2009 a magnificent phoenix display, complex geometric designs, pictograms, mystical codes, intricate mandalas, a detailed jellyfish, a Mayan-like glyph and parallel symbols were formed in British crop fields. Most of these circles were in the vicinity of Stonehenge.

In the 1990s one of the world's most famous UFO researchers was Dr. Steven Greer. This well-known author and lecturer took teams of researchers, equipped with technological devices, to crop circles. Dr. Greer's organization called CSETI uses detectors, flashing light codes and other sophisticated equipment for UFO contacts and communications. This group has successfully communicated with UFOs with multiple witnesses and crowds. Night time stakeouts of crop circle regions had impressive results. The group was able to witness bright, mechanical and intelligently controlled UFOs at crop circles. Some members of the research teams reported witnessing alien beings at the formations.

A major mystery is about why most of the world's nations have no crop circle reports. Some continents report no annual crop circles. Most United States have no crop circles in the news. In the last thirty years that dozens to hundreds of crop circles have appeared annually, over 90 percent have been in the British Isles. Most European nations lack crop circle reports. Some people attribute the great amount of circles in England to the ancient sacred site of Stonehenge as a "cosmic energy vortex." However, many other popular cosmic energy vortices around the world have no crop circle reports.

Since the early 1950s numerous reports of landed flying disks that left circular landing marks have been published. While these circles in crop fields and grasslands are usually not works of art, many have the same, mysterious, inexplicable physical anomalies as geometric and artistic crop circles. One famous English crop circle clearly shows the face of a gray alien.

Many UFO researchers believe that the famous UFO characteristic of "cloaking" is often used at crop circles. Cloaking is an energy field surrounding a spacecraft that makes it invisible to the human range of vision. Eerie sounds have been reported during crop circle manifestations. It is theorized that the UFO occupants use inter-dimensional, powerful, precise light and sound frequencies and beams to create crop circles.

Many crop circles are obviously famous, ancient mystical symbols from temples in past cultures. Other designs are geometrical and mathematical symbols. Some UFO researchers believe that these symbols are coded to raise the levels of enlightenment, psychic ability and spiritual vibrations of the beholders. These symbols are known as Keylontic Codes that program messages into the subconscious. Perhaps, these encoded messages in the mind will be revealed in full consciousness in the future.

Some crop circles are similar to the famous Nazca designs in the Peruvian deserts that can only be viewed from the air. Those ancient, carved formations depict birds, animals and symbols.

In most years about 50 crop circles are reported around the world. The 71 formations reported in 2009 indicate an increase in activity. Once again, most of these circles were in Britain. Only a few circles manifested in Belgium, Poland and the Netherlands and only one reported in the United States.

For excellent photos of 2009 crop circles see Andy Thomas's article in *Nexus* magazine that year. The famous crop circle researcher, author and lecturer Colin Andrews has excellent reference material on the history of crop circles.

It is hoped the crop circles mystery will be solved in the near future. One can only wonder if the governments that hide UFO truths also know the secret facts about crop circles. Are ETs trying to communicate with metaphysical Earth people?

Nonfiction

FIFTY-THREE

The Prophet Peter Deunov

Peter Deunov was a remarkable 19th Century prophet who made many predictions about planetary disasters and a coming golden age. This man continued to make prophecies for many years until he died in 1944. The question is, "How accurate was Peter Deunov? Among the seer's quotes are the following:

"During the passage of time, the consciousness of man has traversed a very long period of obscurity. This phase was called Kali Yuga by the Hindus. We are between two epochs known as the Kali Yuga and the New Era we are entering." These themes and terms are familiar to students of theosophical writings from ancient India like the Vedas.

"A gradual improvement is already occurring in the thoughts, sentiments and acts of humans. Everyone will soon be subjugated to Divine Fire that will purify and prepare them in regard to the New Era. Man will evolve himself to a superior degree of consciousness, indispensable to his entrance to the New Life. That is what one understands by ascension", stated Peter Deunov. Many New Age channelers, alleged ET contactees, and metaphysical researchers came to these same conclusions decades after Peter had died.

"Some decades will pass before this fire will come that will transform the world by bringing it a new moral. This immense wave comes from cosmic space and will inundate the entire Earth. All those that attempt to oppose it will be carried off and transferred elsewhere," stated Peter Deunov. This prophecy sounds much like the many metaphysical authors, psychics, past-life regressionists, UFO researchers and alternative scientists who predict the arrival of Planet X, an asteroid, comet, meteor or dwarf star with an immense wave of fire) to collide with the Earth. Most of these predictions point to 2012 or 2013.

Many of these predictions claim that negative humans will have to reincarnate off this planet and on another world. However, Nostradamus was said to have made a similar prediction for 1999 that was highly publicized, yet never occurred. Famous psychics like Ruth Montgomery and Jeane Dixon predicted the surface of Earth would be destroyed in the 1980s and 1990s. Let us all hope that Peter Deunov will be just as wrong with his cataclysmic prophecies.

Peter Deunov continued, "Although the inhabitants of this planet do not all find themselves at the same degree of evolution, the new wave will be felt by each one of us. This transformation will not only touch the Earth but the entire Cosmos." Peter Deunov added, "The best and only thing that man can do now is turn towards God and improve himself consciously to elevate his vibratory level so as to find himself in harmony with the powerful wave that will soon submerge him."

These quotes are comparable to many ET, Light Being, and Ascended Masters messages which were publicized after Peter's lifetime. These ideas originate from many sources and constitute amazing agreements. David Wilcock, who has been heralded as the reincarnation of Edgar Cayce agrees with those quotes.

Peter Deunov prophesized, "The Fire of which I speak, that accompanies the new conditions offered to our planet, will rejuvenate, purify, reconstruct everything. Matter will be refined. Your hearts will be liberated from anguish, troubles, incertitude and they will become luminous. Everything will be improved, elevated, the thoughts, sentiments and negative acts will be consumed and destroyed."

David Wilcock's website compares to the above quotes. Dolores Cannon, who has performed past life regressions on thousands of clients, found that hundreds of them reported the same revelations. In this case cosmic light beings gave the clients these teachings in classes, between lifetimes, in another dimension. However, this research indicates that this Golden Age of purification, refinement, peace and universal love will occur in a higher dimension or parallel Earth.

Peter Deunov stated, "Your present life is slavery, a heavy prison. Understand your situation and liberate yourself from it. It is really a sorry sight to see so much misleading, so much suffering, so much incapacity to understand where one's true happiness lies. Everything that is around you will soon collapse and disappear. Nothing will be left of this civilization or its perversity. The entire Earth will be shaken and no trace will be left of this erroneous culture that maintains men under the yoke of ignorance."

According to the research from Dolores Cannon, David Wilcock, several psychics and people claiming contacts with benevolent ET races, the negative people of Earth will find themselves in a world disaster that destroys their civilization and dimension. The positive people will find themselves in a Utopia.

Peter Deunov said, "Our solar system is now traversing a region of the Cosmos where a constellation that was destroyed has left its mark, its dusts. This crossing of a contaminated space is a source of poisoning; not only for the inhabitants of the Earth but for all the inhabitants of the other planets of our galaxy. Only the suns are not affected by the influence of this hostile environment. This region is called "the zone of contradictions." Our planet was enclosed in this region for thousands of years; but finally we are approaching the exit of this space of darkness and we are on the point of attaining a more spiritual region where more evolved beings live."

Is this lighter and more spiritual zone of space the "photon belt" at the Galactic Equator that hundreds of metaphysical authors write and lecture about? The photon belt is said to raise our vibrations, awareness and spirituality. The area of space in which the Earth is exiting is said to have kept humanity's vibrations at a lower, denser and more negative vibration of energy. The photon belt will raise the quality of human existence if we tune into it with our more spiritual lifestyle.

"The Earth is now following an ascending movement and everyone should force themselves to harmonize with the currents of the ascension. Those who refuse to subjugate themselves to this orientation will lose the advantage of good conditions that are offered in the future to elevate themselves. They will remain behind in evolution and must wait tens of millions of years for the coming of a new ascending wave. The Earth will soon be swept by extraordinary, rapid waves of Cosmic Electricity."

This quote by Peter Deunov is reminiscent of the Ra Material. Peter Deunov prophesized, "The New Era is that of the sixth race. The sixth race will build itself around the idea of Fraternity. There will be no more conflicts of personal interests; the single aspiration of each one will be to conform to the Law of Love. A new continent will be formed for it. It will emerge from the Pacific, so that the Most High can finally establish His place on this planet."

The idea of 7 root races and the present 5th root race was publicized by Madame Helena Blavatsky in the 1870s to 1880s. This prolific author wrote about planetary cycles of destruction and golden ages that repeat after a certain number of years. This Theosophist predicted we are coming to a transition of a sixth root race to manifest a new Golden Age. Helena Blavatsky claimed she got her information from ancient writings she studied in India like the **Book of Dzyan**, etc.

FIFTY-FOUR

An Interplanetary Adventure

New Zealander, Alec Newald claims that in 1989 he actually traveled to another planet in a solid, physical spaceship! This contactee reported that he was abducted by aliens who were semi-human in appearance. This ten days adventure with friendly space beings is detailed in Alec's book about his journey.

Alec Newald was contacted by Zeena from another planet. Zeena told Alec that "distant common ancestors of ours came to Earth many times; but more important to you was the visit of two million years ago, your time-scale."

Alec said, "These travelers tidied up some earlier attempts to manufacture a race of humanoids on Earth, the end result being Homo sapiens." Zeena said to Alec, "I will not go so far as to say these ancient ancestors of mine were solely responsible for your race, for that was indeed a joint effort of many ETs, all of which at some time have laid claim to manufacturing your race." Zeena continued, "In many ways you have manufactured or at least fine-tuned your own race, and it continues even at this very moment. This is mistakenly called "evolution." Natural progression of the species is a fine turnoff phrase uttered by one of your kind more inquiring minds some years ago. It was thought by many to explain the path of evolution, and there is an end to it. Some of my ancient

Elders stayed with our developing race. Others moved on. From time to time there were conflicts with other ET races as to what was best for one or the other, just as there are conflicts on your planet now, among your own kind. You must understand that Earth is a special place. We would like to live there. But we cannot; indeed we must not interfere with the processes that are happening on your planet right now. That is not to say there are no other ET races that will not interfere and that is why you must have your wits about you."

Zeena responded again. "All knowledge will be made available to your race in good time and in accordance with the laws of evolution." Zeena continued, "A force of darkness altered your DNA. It crippled you and stunted you and set you back many thousands of years. This dark force is the enemy of enlightenment. We and others are indeed benevolent to your race, as we are connected. We find that there is a need to teach you more about the dark forces that permeate you. You would do well by your people if you take great heed of this lesson and pass on your findings to those of your kind who would listen."

Zeena went on to communicate more with Alec. She said, "The reason behind so many abductions occurring on your planet over the last few years of your time is that this is the last chance for our race and other races of ETs with problems similar to ours to interact with you as a race before you change to a form that will no longer be of use to us."

Zeena told Alec that her race must breed a race with stronger limbs and oxygen processing units. He had learned that her race will evolve with intelligence. However, their bodies were flimsy. They had thick arms and legs and very thin bodies. Their heads and eyes were large in comparison to their bodies. They were benevolent. They need a new place to live on another planet. Their planet is dying out. Oxygen is scarce. Alec Newald learned about their philosophy of life and their life style. He developed an open mind about these ETs.

Nonfiction

FIFTY-FIVE

California—Land of Resources

California has more people than any other state of the United States of America. Many visitors and new residents are attracted by California's outdoor life. The warm, dry climate of southern California permits outdoor recreation almost all the year around.

California ranks first among the states in manufacturing. More goods are made in California than in any other state. California leads in the manufacture of electronic equipment. Its products also include aircraft and food products as baked goods and wines. California leads in mining as well. Its fields of oil and natural gas yield thousands of barrels of fuel a day.

California ranks first among all the states in agriculture. The Central Valley extends 450 miles where fruits, nuts and vegetables are the leading region in America. California is a center of the motion pictures and television industries. Its entertainment products are distributed throughout the world.

California has four of our nation's twenty largest cities known as Los Angeles, San Diego, San Jose and San Francisco. The state capital is Sacramento, another large city. The international airports at Los Angeles and San Francisco are among the busiest in the world. The ports along California's Pacific Coast make this state a leading area for international trade with Latin America and Asia.

Hundreds of computer and electronic companies have their headquarters in California research laboratories, computer companies and engineering firms cluster around universities in and near the largest cities. Scientists and engineers from the universities use computers to do research. They use their brain power.

California covers a larger area than any other state except Alaska and Texas. The high Sierra Nevada rises near the shore of the Pacific Ocean in the west. Thick forests of Douglas-firs and giant redwood trees cover the coast ranges and the Klamath Mountains in the northwest. Barren deserts stretch across the southeast.

The Spaniards were the first Europeans to colonize California. Franciscan friars from Spain established the first of a chain of missions there in 1769. California is called the Golden State. Its gold fields attracted thousands of miners, known as the "Forty-Niners" during the gold rush of 1849. California is known as the sunshine state because the sun shines brilliantly.

The highest temperature ever recorded in the United States is 134 degrees in Death Valley on July 10, 1913. The lowest elevation in the Western Hemisphere is located near Badwater in Death Valley. It lies 282 feet below sea level. The world's tallest living tree rises 368 feet in the Tall Trees Grove in Redwood National Park. The first cable car street railway system was installed in San Francisco in 1873. The General Sherman tree in Sequoia National Park is one of the world's largest living things. It has a circumference of 103 feet at the base and rises 275 feet. This tree is estimated to be about 2,500 years old.

Beverly Hills, a fashionable city near the Hollywood district of Los Angeles, has many beautiful homes with swimming pools. The first synchronized sound cartoon was Walt Disney's Steamboat Willie, produced in Hollywood in 1928. It featured Mickey Mouse. The Golden Gate Bridge spans a channel at the entrance of San Francisco Bay. One of the world's longest suspension bridges has a total length of 8,981 feet.

Yosemite National Park lies in the Sierra Nevada in east-central California. Several national parks preserve the natural beauty of the state's scenic mountains, valleys, lakes and forests.

Chief products in California are almonds, beef cattle, cotton, grapes, greenhouse and nursery products, hay, lettuce, milk, strawberries and tomatoes. Manufacturing products are chemical, computer and electronic products, fabricated metal products, food products and fabricated transportation equipment. Mining resources are boron, cement, natural gas, petroleum, sand and gravel.

In the late 1700's and early 1800's, Franciscan friars taught farming, weaving and other crafts to the Indians of California. A few small schools were established in the region. However, most children of the early settlers in California received instruction from private teachers. The state's first public high school opened in 1856 in San Francisco. In 1910, California established in Fresno the first tax-supported junior college in the United States. An 11 member state Board of Education sets policies for California's elementary and secondary school system. The members of the board are appointed by the governor, subject to the approval of the state Senate. Members serve four-year terms, except for one student representative, who serves one year. The California Department of Education provides assistance to the state's local school districts and county offices of education, and it divides state and federal funds among them. An elected superintendent of public instruction heads the department.

California State University is the largest state supported system of four year and graduate-level education in the United States. It has more than 20 campuses and about 400,000 students. Another state-supported university, the University of California, has 10 campuses and more than 208,000 students. California also has an outstanding system of community colleges. A master plan, which was approved by the State Legislature in 1960, provides for the orderly expansion of the system of state colleges and universities.

California's outstanding public library system was founded in 1909. Today, public libraries exist throughout the state. All types of libraries in California have formed and informed cooperative arrangements between them for sharing resources. The University of California at Berkeley has the largest university library in the state.

Places to visit in California are Disneyland, The Getty Center, Hearst Castle, Knott's Berry Farm, California Missions, Monterey

Bay, National Marine Sanctuary, Monterey Peninsula, Redwood Highway, San Diego Zoo, Parklands, National Forests, State parks and monuments, Tournament of Roses Parade in Pasadena, Old Spanish Days Fiesta in Santa Barbara, Hollywood Walk of the Stars, The legendary "Sunset Strip", Palm Springs and Yosemite.

California's two largest rivers are the Sacramento and the San Joaquin. The Sacramento River rises near Mount Shasta and flows south through the Central Valley. The San Joaquin rises in the Sierra Nevada and flows northwest through the Central Valley. The two rivers meet northeast of San Francisco, and flow west into San Francisco Bay. The place where the two rivers meet is the Delta, a maze of channels and islands. The Colorado River forms the borders between southern California and Arizona. It is an important source of water for Southern California cities. Water from the Colorado is also used to irrigate desert farmlands. Yosemite National Park has several of the highest waterfalls in North America. Ribbon Falls is the highest on the continent.

California has about 8,000 lakes. Lake Tahoe is the deepest lake in depth. Most of the desert lakes east of the Sierra contain dissolved minerals that give the water a disagreeable taste. Potash, salt and other minerals are taken from Owens Lake, Searles Lake and other dry or partly dry lakes in this region. The Salton Sea is a large, shallow lake in southern California. It was formed between 1905 and 1907 by floodwaters from the Colorado River.

California has redwood trees. Forests cover about 40 percent of California. Softwood trees make up most of the forests. These trees include cedars, firs, hemlocks, giant sequoias, pines as well as redwoods. The most common hardwood trees are oaks. Desert plants cover much of the southeastern section of the state. These plants included burroweeds, creosote bushes, indigo bushes, Joshua trees and several kinds of cactuses. Desert wildflowers include desert evening primrose and sand verbena. Patches of chaparral (thick and often thorny shrubs) and small trees cover the foothills.

Desert wildlife in California includes coyotes, lizards and rattlesnakes. Beavers, bears, deer, foxes, minks, muskrats, rabbits, wildcats, wolverines and a few mountain sheep roam the mountain and forest areas. Small herds of pronghorns and elk are found in the northern part of the state. California game birds include ducks, geese, grouse, mourning dove, quail and turkey. Game fishes in the state's streams include black bass, salmon, striped bass and trout. Abalone, clams, crabs, shrimps, lobsters, oysters, scallops and other shellfish are found along the California coast.

California ranks among the leading states in commercial fishing. Its annual fish catch is valued at more than $140 million. Crabs are the most valuable catch. Squid are the second most Catch in the state and California has a larger squid catch than any other state. Other commercially important seafood catches include lobster, oysters, tablefish, salmon, sardines, sea urchins, shrimp, swordfish and tuna. California's fish catches also include anchovies, halibut, herring, mackerel, rockfish and sole.

Nonfiction

FIFTY-SIX

Become Well Educated

Becoming well educated is a valuable experience. The more a person develops his or her awareness of cultural experiences, literature, the Arts, environmental awareness and social and scientific research, etc, he or she becomes more educated.

A well-educated person learns to choose between different options. There may be a variety of answers to a question. There are different options. A well educated person is usually well rounded and open-minded. The more one can learn about specific subjects the more understanding and awareness one can develop.

Well educated individuals usually are able to receive better occupations. They may earn higher annual salaries. Well educated individuals may think deeper and may be more enlightened because they are well read and have more intellectual awareness.

A well educated person is capable of communicating effectively. He or she is able to write well and think about what they read. They have selected a variety of reference books, research materials and visual materials and aids. They know how to use college as well as public libraries effectively to do research and to read many resource and enrichment books.

A well educated person usually adapts better in his or her environment. He or she usually becomes a leader in the community, town or city. Well educated individuals usually contribute to their culture.

Fiction

FIFTY-SEVEN

Country Life

Country life can be very special because the air usually is fresher. Many views of the countryside are beautiful to observe. There are colorful meadows, forests, verdant-green valleys with wild flowers and green grass. The countryside is magnificent and splendid to dwell in. Many flowers and clover grow in meadows as well.

Dolores Williams lived in the country. She enjoyed walking in the woods near her home. The eucalyptus trees and fir trees smelled quite fragrant. Dolores was able to sit in the woods under tall, shady trees. She looked up through the trees at rays of sunlight. These rays of light gleamed through the closely spaced trees. The sunshine felt warm and pleasant.

Dolores often went for walks in the woods and valleys near where she lived. She observed bark peeling off tree trunks. A strong aroma emanated from the wide trunk trees. Pine, spruce, oak and fir trees were growing in fields and hillsides. Dolores appreciated the majestic beauty of these trees.

Frequently, Dolores sat out in her beautiful garden. She witnessed violet and yellow flowers blooming. She saw wild yellow sour grass growing everywhere. Bees buzzed as they flew around from flower to flower. Dolores was mystified at the lovely sight. She was fascinated how bees moved around from flower to flower to gather nectar to take back to their beehive. Bees literally sucked in nectar with their mouths. Then they continued to gather more and more nectar which will bring more and more flower substance to their beehive.

Dolores realized that the ecosystem is necessary because creatures, insects and plants are interdependent in order to survive. Bees depend on nectar to bring to the beehive to make honey. Squirrels depend on nuts to fall on the ground. They collect the nuts for food. Rabbits scurry through meadows and woodlands to look for vegetables and grass to eat in meadows. Birds hunt for seeds and shrubs and grass to eat. Fish, swimming in nearby ponds, depend on water plants and small pieces of plankton as well as water insects to eat.

Dolores enjoyed taking long walks and hikes in meadows and in the valleys nearest to her home. In fact, she took a long, daily walk in order to exercise as well as to enjoy nature. She loved to sniff wild flowers such as lupines, wild poppies and sour grass flowers. She stopped to watch various birds perching in trees and plucking seeds and grass. She watched rabbits hopping around nibbling grass and shrubs. They also nibbled on plant roots.

Dolores was able to become close to Nature because she lived in the country. She passed old barns as well as hay stacks. She liked to climb up hay stacks to rest after walking for quite a while. She gazed up at the blue sky and passing clouds as she lay in the hay stack.

While Dolores went walking along country roads and pathways she experienced raindrops coming down. She became wet because of the rain falling quickly to the Earth. She took a hot bath once she returned to her home.

Dolores felt happier and freer because she lived in the country. She was able to become well acquainted with neighbors and villagers where she lived. She decided to remain in the country to enjoy Nature and a small village life.

Nonfiction

FIFTY-EIGHT

The Mysteries of Shambhala

For many thousands of years there have been legends of ancient writings about a subterranean race of super humans, giants, adepts, initiates, masters and cosmic beings living under the Himalayas. Several explorers have written books claiming they found or entered tunnels into this mysterious kingdom. Other legendary underground realms in the Himalayas like Shangri-La and Agharti are said to be related to Shambhala. These mystical abodes are said to be under Tibet, Kashmir and Mongolia.

The legends, old writings and more modern books tell us that Shambhala was colonized by an advanced extraterrestrial race many millions of years ago. Some writings refer to this race as the Elder Race. These sources also claim that a race of very advanced Lemurians from the Lost Continent of Mu, as well as a root race from the Lost Continent of Thule, fled world cataclysms and colonized Shambhala. These civilizations chose to remain hidden from the violent, aggressive, warlike and conquering cultures on the surface. By remaining secret and obscure the people of Shambhala could advance peacefully, harmoniously, technologically and spiritually with no interference. With millions of years to advance their civilization, Shambhala became far more evolved than surface humanity.

There have been many UFO sightings in the Himalayas and some authors and explorers believe these craft originate in Shambhala. Many writers claim that masters and avatars sometime emerge from underground to teach humanity spiritual principals and metaphysics.

Writings from the Himalayas tell us that Buddha and Lao Tzu both visited the Valley Of The Immortals in the Kingdom of Shambhala. In ancient times parts of this subterranean kingdom were said to have extended to the surface of the Earth into very remote valleys. These surface temples were so difficult to hike to over the rugged, ice-packed mountains that outsiders usually failed to complete the journey. The few outsiders who were able to make this rugged, dangerous and exhausting adventure were turned back before entering sacred areas.

Details about Shambhala and its inhabitants are found in the ancient TIBETAN BOOK OF THE DEAD, THE BARDO THODOL, and the SOUL DOCTRINE by C. Chan. Several volumes of the largest encyclopedia in the world, the YNF-LO-TA-TIEN, tell of Shambhala. More information on this subject is in CRIMSON SNOW-HEAPS IN THE HIMALAYAS by Sergy C. Tatyang from 1925. Another source about Shambhala is HIMALAYAS-ABODE OF LIGHT, written by the famous, Russian explorer Nicholas Roerich. In the 1700s the third Panchen Lama wrote ROAD TO SHAMBHALA. There are also references in the 19th Century writings of Madame Helena Blavatsky. The thousand year old Vyshenski Upspenski manuscript allegedly tells about Shambhala. THE LAND OF NO GRASS AND NO WATER, by Jia Chun Pingwa gives many details of this underground kingdom.

Many of these old writings tell about huge libraries that preserved all the lost histories of Earth for millions of years. Scholars say that most of the past histories of Earth on the surface were destroyed when invading armies burned the ten biggest libraries of antiquity. However, underground initiates are said to have preserved secret copies of this lost history.

Cecelia Frances Page

These underground archives are said to contain huge storehouses of fabulous art, treasures, artifacts and other items dating from the origins of humanity. Some writings state that only seven people from the surface of the Earth are allowed to visit Shambhala each year. These people were trained to be spiritual teachers for mankind.

Several metaphysical and theosophical writings claim that there are similar underground, secret retreats of great cosmic beings below Mount Shasta, in California, as well as beneath the Andes Mountains and other sacred zones. These subterranean abodes are said to be connected to each other by tunnels.

In the last sixty years the United States, Russian, Norwegian, British and other governments have built secret, underground bases. These projects may survive planetary cataclysms and a possible nuclear war. Could the ancients have built underground sanctuaries too, in order to escape disasters?

Nonfiction

FIFTY-NINE

Giants Still Exist on Earth

For centuries there have been native tales of living giants in the Solomon Islands. There have also been sightings of the giants in the 20th Century by a crew of 30 witnesses at the same time, the Premier and Finance Minister of Guadalcanal and other witnesses. Footprints from giant human feet have been witnessed as additional evidence.

Sightings and encounters with giants are in the histories of most ancient civilizations and religions. The Bible claims there were once giants on Earth. Stone staircases, furniture, seats and doors made for humans of giant size were reported to have been explored in Bolivia. Skeletons and mummies of giants were found in France in the 1500s-1700s and in the United States desert southwest in the 19th Century. These findings were reported in newspapers and books. Remains of giants were reportedly excavated in the Andes Mountains and were described by the Indians in Peru and Bolivia in the 16th Century. So, could there still be living giants today in the Solomon Islands?

Witnesses described these giants as over ten feet tall with long brown or red hair, bulging red eyes, a flat nose, hairy body and a wide mouth. Another race of hairy dwarf humans is also said to exist in these dense rainforests. There is also a third species that appears to

Cecelia Frances Page

be a hybrid that had mated with human natives. There are so many natives who have testified on these sightings and for so many years that the evidence of giants is massive.

Skeptics may ask how giants can survive undetected by anthropologists? According to the tribes in the Solomon Islands, these huge people live in an extensive network of hidden caverns and tunnels below ground in dense jungles. There is said to even be a city of giants beneath Mount Tatuva where there have been far too many sightings to ignore. A burial ground for giants has been found full of huge skeletons in Kwara'ae.

Most of the islands in this chain have sightings of giants but most of them are reported on Choiseul and Guadalcanal. Mining expeditions have encountered evidence.

According to extensive explorations of South Pacific islands by Colonel James Churchward and numerous followers—these islands are the remaining mountain peaks of a lost civilization called Mu (Lemuria). These researchers found monolithic, extremely ancient, stone buildings on many islands across the Pacific that they concluded came from Mu. The famous explorer and archaeological researcher David Hatcher Childress also explored some of these islands and speculated they could be from this submerged civilization. Mu (Lemuria) is said to have been home to a race of giants!

Mysterious stone buildings, obelisks and ancient hieroglyphs were found in the land of the giants in the Solomon Islands. According to the famous 19th Century explorer Helena P. Blavatsky—giants inhabited these islands and others in the Pacific when they were part of the Lemurian civilization. This prolific writer claimed to have read very ancient writings in temples in India, Tibet and East Asia and found information on the giants of Lemuria. This civilization was said to have been mostly submerged by earthquakes and volcanic eruptions leaving Pacific Islands on the surface. Helena wrote in her books on Theosophy that these giants were an extinct prehistoric root race. However, could these giants in the Solomon Islands be *surviving* Lemurians?

Hikers can see these stone monuments on Mount Mala on Malaita in the Solomons. The local natives refer to the giants in the area as "Ramos." One bone about eight feet long was found here! *Nexus* magazine from Australia did an excellent article on these giants, written by Marius Boirayon. His book ***Soloman Islands Mysteries*** is highly recommended for discovering many more details.

The Third Root Race was known to be giants. They lived long ago. Giants who still exist may be descendants of the Third Root Race. This race of humans was described in the ancient ***Book of Dzyan*** from India, said to be over 5,000 years old. Giants have also been reported in Asia where they are called "Yeti."

In Florida there are swampland areas where Big Foot giants exist. They have been seen wandering near the trees which exist in shady swamps. They leave their large footprints as they roam about.

Giants have been seen in remote areas of the Himalaya Mountains and isolated regions of China. Bigfoot creatures appear to be a different species than Solomon Island giants with different eye color, facial features and considerably more hair. Giants still exist in isolated areas around the world.

Nonfiction

SIXTY

Wild Sailboard Adventures

A sailboard resembles a surfboard with a sail attached, which includes a mast and booms. The booms keep the sail from flapping out of control and are used to hang on and steer. Out of millions of sailboarders (windsurfers) about 98% only are found in lakes, bays, harbors, lagoons and other *flat water*. Only a small fraction of windsurfers have the very advanced skills and courage to perform in ocean waves, risking terrifying dangers and accidents.

Maui Island, Hawaii is considered to be the ***ultimate*** place to windsurf in the world, because of its reputation for frequently strong winds, big surf, winter's warm air and water, lots of great sailing spots with frequently favorable wind directions. Maui is the home of most of the champions and pros and the main training ground for the best European windsurfers. Maui windsurfers have ridden waves over 50 feet high at Jaws, where the ***biggest surfing waves in the world*** are located. Maui sailboarders also sail across the ocean between different Hawaiian islands where they risk extremely strong currents and high seas. Dozens of boats and kayaks have sunk or disappeared in these channels, as well as vanishing windsurfers.

Steve Omar was a well-known freestyle windsurfer on Maui who invented some very difficult trick maneuvers. He was a featured windsurfer in numerous videos, newspapers, international magazines and national TV. As Editor, owner and columnist for **Maui Sailboarder** magazine and writer for some Maui newspapers, Steve interviewed World Cup champions, World Speed Record holders and other super-stars about their personal wipeouts, injuries and disasters at sea. However, Steve eventually became his own victim of many of these types of wipeouts and disasters!

There were days when the winds became so strong even the famous pros could *not* sail. One afternoon gale force winds "suddenly" blasted into a crowded windsurfing beach. Steve was blown off his sailboard in a "catapult", when the body is like a 'sling-shot' through the air, as the booms are ripped out of both hands and the sail flips with overwhelming force. The windsurfer is slammed into the water at high speed. Steve looked around and *every* windsurfer he saw in the ocean had been blown off their sailboards—an estimated 50 sailors including many famous pros! All the windsurfers had to swim all the way to the beach as they dragged up to 100 pounds of the equipment through raging riptides. On the beach the wind was so powerful it blew the roofs off some nearby houses and blew down trees! Sailboards still attached to their sail rigs were seen blowing down the beach like tumbleweed.

Windsurfers attempted to detach their sails to take them apart and move their sailboards to their vehicles. However, wind gusts tore the sails out of their hands. Flying booms and sails hit other windsurfers walking down the beach, even in the head. Some of the rigged sails were blown up into trees that people had to climb to retrieve. I once heard of a windsurfer knocked out while on the beach by a flying mast and sail and I saw sail rigs crash into cars.

However, a windier date came to the Maui Beach Center location, where Steve once managed a windsurfing and surfing school and did rentals. Tradewinds became so strong they wrapped around both ends of the West Maui Mountains and collided with gale force from *opposite* directions. The result was whirling mini-tornados called "dust devils" that came across the park to the beach center scattering debris. The gusts blew the surfboards out of the rental rack and sent them flying through the air and tumbling down the beach! Fully rigged, huge, beginner sailboards were tumbling down the beach with the sails still attached. The wind blew a big beach umbrella, rental gear, rafts, surfboards, sails, snorkel equipment and other items across the beach and into the ocean. A cashier was counting money and gusts blew it out of his hands and the bills went flying off all over the beach. A large boat on the beach was blown over on its side.

Meanwhile, Steve Omar was windsurfing alone next to this disaster. After years of intense practice, Omar was able to ride the waves and hold on to his sail and continue sailing. However, a whirling dust devil that had just caused damage on the beach entered the ocean and headed directly toward Steve, who was unable to sail fast enough to escape the collision. A waterspout tornado slammed into the sail and Steve was catapulted. After surfacing the sailboard and attached sail were seen tumbling through the air like a tumbleweed. The escape was to swim to shore through the raging water and riptides over dangerous, shallow, sharp coral that sliced his feet and leg.

Another day Hurricane Iniki slammed into the Hawaiian Islands and caused massive destruction on Kauai. The side of the hurricane brushed Lahaina, Maui as Steve ate breakfast in a waterfront restaurant. A newspaper reported there was 20 to 30 foot hurricane surf breaking in Lahaina. Steve was watching this surf from the restaurant, as well as sinking boats anchored offshore and two surfers getting rescued by a helicopter. A gust of wind blasted into the restaurant and blew table-ware off the tables. Servers freaked out as debris flew across the dining room. So, Steve asked the waitress for his bill and told her it was "time to go windsurfing!" People said, "You're crazy!"

These waves were so big that they washed across the coastal highway, flooded the parks, washed into the dining tables of the next door restaurant, flooded the parking lot, washed into cars and crashed yachts and fishing boats into beaches, reefs and rocks. Steve sailed out at the Lahaina Harbor where big waves were breaking over the top of the large, boulders breakwater that was *supposed* to protect the boats *inside* the harbor. However, the surf washed over the break wall and crashed into some boats inside the harbor!

Steve successfully windsurfed about a half dozen of the smaller waves that were still considered " big", by the standards of most windsurfers. As he windsurfed out he was able to fly up in the air off the tops of waves without crashing. In the air fishing boats and yachts anchored nearby could be seen sinking. Some of these very rough, crashing waves towered over his sail.

Although it was gale force winds and getting stronger Steve continued to windsurf. Eventually the wind became too strong and Omar was blown off his board in a catapult. The seas were frothing and a set of big waves plowed over. Steve was held underwater and tossed like a rag doll in a washing machine, as his sailboard was lost and thrashed on the boulders of the breakwater. The big surf and rocks broke the mast in half, broke the booms, ripped the sail to shreds and destroyed the sailboard. Steve fought a raging riptide current as he narrowly missed getting slammed into the boulders. Meanwhile, another sailboard he left on the beach had been washed across the park and to the parking lot. Steve staggered out of the water and viewed all the damage and destruction. His beach concession had been totally destroyed! Some of the equipment was crashed on an exposed coral reef on the other side of the lagoon and some was buried in the sand. Some equipment was never found. Steve lost his business, yet was rewarded with a thrilling day of windsurfing! He had survived the huge waves and gales of a hurricane.

Most inter-island windsurfers sailed to Molokai Island which was dangerous but fun. In interviews Steve wrote about some windsurfers who broke down **between** Maui and Molokai who ended up spending the night at sea. The "Molokai Express" current was as strong as a raging river and it was impossible to paddle **against** it to an island. Some of these guys were shipwrecked at a remote beach on Lanai Island and had to be rescued. Bill Whidden's sail rig broke, and he spent a dark night tied to his drifting sailboard. Bill awoke on a wave being crashed into a coral reef on Lanai. There were reports of some windsurfers who vanished without a trace!

However, it was considered so dangerous to windsurf to Lanai Island that nearly all windsurfers refused to try. Steve had only met one windsurfer who sailed to Lanai and that guy was the World

Speed Champion! Another victim of this dangerous crossing was Mark Angulo who got to Lanai "accidentally." Steve had been sailing about a mile off Lahaina when the wind totally stopped and he had to swim to shore where he had seen sharks. The sail of another windsurfer was much further out to sea to the south. Mark had also run out of wind but was caught in the notorious "Molokai Express" current and sucked miles out to sea. The current heads between the islands of Lanai and Kahoolawe. A Coast Guard spokesman said that "If you miss those islands, the next stop is Tahiti!" A number of boats and a kayaker had vanished out there, too. Tahiti was over 2,000 miles away!

Mark ended up spending the night on his sailboard drifting in the current until he crashed into a beach near the tip of Lanai. He had to hike down a long and deserted beach to Club Lanai---the only civilization on the east coast of Lanai. Because Mark Angulo was a world cup windsurfing champion and among the best in the world. It could happen to the best!

After interviewing Mark, Omar decided to take up the challenge. The theory was that one of the several tourist boats that sailed from Lahaina to Lanai could come to the rescue in an accident. The idea was to leave in the morning during a steady wind increase forecast. Steve set out alone and was approximately half way to Lanai when the strongest wind gusts he ever encountered slammed into his sail. He was catapulted off into raging seas. Dark, black rain clouds were approaching from the north as the big gale storm came too early. The weather man was wrong!

Soon there were seas estimated at 20 feet slamming into the sail and board as Steve helplessly drifted in the Molokai Express current. It was impossible to sail in gusts of nearly hurricane force. He was floating around in the ocean in the strongest current he had ever seen. There were no boats to rescue anybody. It was so windy that the Coast Guard reportedly closed the ocean to boating and refused to let them leave the harbors.

This part of the ocean was known for big sharks and whales. A herd of whales was heading on a collision course with Steve as he floated helplessly, and the seas were so big it appeared they couldn't even see him. These whales came so close to hitting him that this was the scariest part of the disaster. Three windsurfers Steve interviewed had already collided with whales. One of them broke her sailboard in half and another was attacked by the whale. The other guy was in the Molokai Express channel when a whale surfaced underneath his sailboard and lifted him out of the water!

After this narrow escape it was nearing sundown. Steve began to wonder if it was his turn to get in an article about disappearing in this zone and he could easily die. However, he kept calm and eventually saw nearby land in the mist filled air. The wind was blowing so much spray off the waves, it was difficult to see anything. With all his strength and a burst of adrenaline, Steve water-started his body up on his board. In overpowering winds the lower the crouch and the further you lean back, the easier to hang on to the sail rig. The technique is to drag the butte in the water and lean back so far the back slaps the water. In this position waves washed over Steve and knocked him off a few more times. However, he was barely able to hold on to the booms with all high might and blast into a deserted beach.

Steve was now lost at the edge of a beach and jungle. He knew that the only civilization on this coast was a small bar, hammocks and picnic tables at Club Lanai. There were no roads along the coastline and it was densely vegetated. Steve knew Club Lanai was closed and deserted at night and there would be no shelter from the storm. It was too windy to sail south in the lagoon. Luckily the winter ocean was warm and, though it was stormy it was warm and humid. Steve gazed at the nearby coconut palm trees bending in the blasting winds. He began pushing his sailboard along the edge of the lagoon when two Hawaiian fishermen ran out of the woods and came to the rescue.

These guys were from another island and had been camping out to fish when the gale hit. They brought out water, food, blankets and a warm coat. Steve said, "I remember just lying on my back on the ground in this raging storm, gazing up at the palm trees and watching coconuts and branches flying through the air. It was so surreal it seemed like I was dreaming it all. But the force of the storm on my body told me it was all too real."

The Hawaiians decided this was a bad risk, so one of them decided to hike down the coast to Club Lanai to try to find a boat for a rescue. However, he returned saying there was only one boat and the captain refused to risk sailing in this gale. Spending the night in the woods in one of the biggest storms of 1997 did not seem like a good idea for a windsurfer in total exhaustion and who was shaking all over in a daze.

However, a big motorized boat suddenly came cruising up the lagoon. The captain disembarked and checked out Steve and decided he had to get him back to safety on Maui in spite of the risks. So Omar left his sailboard and rig on Lanai and got on a small motorboat to ride out to the big boat in the lagoon. Waves washed over the boat and drenched Steve and the captain, who had to climb up a ladder on to the deck. On the way to Maui big waves broke over the bow of the big boat and sprayed the windows and cabin. The captain had a very worried look on his face and commented that "I hope we make it." Steve pointed to the frothing seas and waves and replied, "I made it on a tiny sailboard. How do you think I made it?" The captain was totally amazed. Yet, somehow the two made it to Maui after a very dangerous crossing in the type of conditions that had sank dozens of fishing boats and yachts in those waters.

Another time Steve tried to windsurf to Lanai, got about half way there and the wind totally stopped. He got caught in the Molokai Express current, missed Lanai and was getting sucked toward Tahiti. It was getting dark and there were no boats in sight. Paddling only went backwards. If it got dark it would have been a likely death. Right before sunset a fishing boat went speeding by over a mile away as Steve yelled and hooted. The craft kept going and it looked like the last chance was over. Suddenly, the boat made a u-turn and came to the rescue. The captain was alarmed that anybody would be in this zone because this was where Hawaiians "fished for sharks." Sunset is dinner time for sharks. Steve was drifting in a shark breeding zone!

Before the surf spot of Jaws became known in the 1990s—the biggest waves on Maui were usually at the Kings Reefs that broke on the horizon! These waves are so big, powerful, tricky, dangerous and far out to sea that most of the pros even refused to go there when the surf was big. It was so difficult to find any windsurfer that had the nerve to sail those 20-40 foot high waves that Steve often had to sail it alone.

There were also hidden, extremely shallow reefs of razor sharp coral that were under swirling whitewater out of site. One day Steve caught a wave and was racing to the bottom of it to make a turn. Half way down this crashing wave a coral reef suddenly appeared at the bottom of the wave! The razor sharp coral was sticking out of the water! It was too late to get off the wave which was breaking very fast. Steve did a turn and heard the coral tearing into the bottom of his sailboard ripping the fiberglass to shreds and breaking off the fin. So, Steve bent over and laid his sail out horizontally and dove on top of it clinging to the booms. The wave crashed on top and dragged the equipment across the reef with Steve on top of the sail. The wipeout broke the mast in half, destroyed the booms and ripped the sail to shreds. The equipment drifted into the calm lagoon and Steve swam to the beach and hiked back to his car without an injury. The secret was martial arts training on how to fall.

The surf can get big very fast and with little warning. One day Steve had a windsurfing lesson to teach at another beach several miles down the coast on the north shore of Maui. However, the vehicle and trailer to drive the equipment broke down at the windsurfing shop by the beach. Steve had prided himself on never being late for, or missing a lesson customer. The other instructors were not in the shop and there were no vehicles big enough to carry all this equipment available. So, Steve decided to windsurf to work like he had done on several occasions. However, he did not know that the surf had become so huge that contest officials had cancelled the nearby World Cup Windsurfing Championships! The waves were so big that many pro champions could not even get out through the surf!

Steve was in too much of a hurry to check the surf which had been mellow the last few days. Arriving at the shoreline there were ten foot waves crashing right on the beach in an exploding shorebreak! Gazing out to sea the whitewater went all the way to the horizon! It was the biggest surf Steve had ever encountered. So, the plan was to wait for a break in the shorebreak, enter the water full speed and zigzag and dodge the waves through channels—all the way to the other beach. This technique had worked in 20-25 foot surf.

However, about a mile out to sea Steve began to estimate that there were 30 or possibly 40 foot waves! Surf broke all the way across the channels. The riptides were like raging rivers and the winds were blasting strong enough to blow sand down the beaches. Steve would be sailing out and see a group of monster waves heading toward his board. He said, "These huge waves are about to crash. You have to make an *instant* decision to u-turn or jump and the wrong decision could kill you. A jibe is a fast u-turn and you have to figure out where 135 degrees downwind is in a split second. On that course you can out-run the wave. If you mis-estimate that course and turn between 91 and 120 degrees downwind the huge wave will catch up and crash on you. We had to learn those degree angles by feeling the wind pressure on our sails. If you mistakenly turn up wind you get thrashed. Dozens of huge waves will push you deep underwater as you are tumbled around like a rag in a huge washing machine. It is quite easy to drown. When you surface more big waves are breaking on top of you, so it takes extreme endurance. You look around and your sailboard is nowhere in sight and can be a half mile away lost in the whitewater. I've seen abandoned sailboards without sails and just sails floating around out there and could not find the sailor! The swim in can be over a mile through thrashing whitewater, blasting winds, and currents as strong as river riptides. If you get in a channel, these currents can suck you over a mile out to sea in an area famous for sharks."

Steve Omar said, "The other instant decision is to try to fly over the top of the approaching wave called "jumping." The technique is to race up the wave full speed and launch as high as 20 to 40 feet into the air. This jump must be done *before* the wave breaks on you! If you mis-judge when the wave will break and get half way up it and it crashes on you---it is one of the worst imaginable wipeouts.

I have seen windsurfers get almost to the top of the wave, it breaks on them and they fall over backwards and upside down. The sail lands on the windsurfer's head, the wave crashes on top of it and pins the sailor under the sail. Meanwhile, the sailboard, sail rig and sailor get tumbled to the bottom of the wave that caves in on top of this tangled mess. The frequent result is a broken mast, torn up sail, damaged sailboard and a long, dangerous swim."

Once high in the air, if the windsurfer steers too far downwind he will get catapulted and blasted off into the air. The sailor will land in the water hoping the sailboard will not land on his head. "I know windsurfers who got catapulted up in the air and their entire bodies fell through their sails! This wipeout left a big hole in the sail and one pro broke his neck. If the windsurfer turns too far upwind while in the air he will stall, lose power and fall to the surface upside down and backwards. Skills at steering in the air, in very strong winds, take years of consistent practice and hundreds of trial wipeouts."

High in the air the windsurfer can see the approaching big waves and prepare to land. The method of landing is critical. If the windsurfer lands with the sailboard horizontal to the water the force can break the board in two pieces or snap an ankle or two! Both feet in footstraps are used for control and the sailboard must land with the front end up and the back end facing the water so it skips like a stone across the water. If the sailboard is pointing too far downwind on this landing the windsurfer gets catapulted. If the windsurfer lands too far upwind, between 45 and 0 degrees, the sail will land on his head and he falls over backwards in front of the huge, crashing wave. If the landing is successful, the instant decision on whether or not to jump or u-turn and flee the next wave is critical. Landing the jump is a huge loss of speed to fly up the next wave—that is usually less than ten seconds away from a collision course. Fast u-turns in choppy, churning water take a huge amount of skill. If the turn is too slow the next wave will thrash the windsurfer.

Steve's years of nearly daily practice paid off as he zig-zagged in and out dodging huge, broken walls of whitewater and jumped dozens of these huge waves. Meanwhile, the wind became so strong and overpowering he could barely hold on to his sail rig with all his strength. It was far windier a mile out than on the beach. Once out past all the biggest waves, Steve turned on the more difficult downwind course and headed about four miles up the coast to the other beach. He was so over-powered by strong gusts that his arms and fingers ached in pain trying to hold on, yet a wipeout there could end in drowning. Once off the other beach, Steve caught a huge wave and windsurfed it for an estimated half mile into a lagoon. He raced in to the beach full speed and found the windsurfing student waiting on the beach for the lesson. Steve had made it to his lesson on time! However, he had to tell the beginner student that it was not a good day to learn to windsurf!

As Steve arrived on the beach he met former World Champion Peter Cabrinha entering the water and asking how it was out there? After being told that Steve had sailed all the way down the coast from the windsurfing shop in those monster waves and blasting winds, Peter said he was amazed at that accomplishment. Peter had just come from the World Cup contest beach at Hookipa, and said the surf was so big that the pro windsurfers could not even get out there! The contest had been cancelled that day.

Steve became the "Windsurfer Professor at Maui Community College, teaching semesters of beginner to pro windsurfing and how to avoid the mistakes he made by teaching himself to sailboard. Later, Steve had his own windsurfing radio show on Hawaii's popular FM-101 Radio heard on 4 islands. Steve invented extremely difficult, new windsurfing tricks and maneuvers and was sponsored with free equipment, worth thousands of dollars for doing freestyle exhibitions in videos, magazines and "live." He had destroyed thousands of dollars of equipment, so freebies kept him sailing!

Nonfiction

SIXTY-ONE

Underground Egyptian Temple Discovered in the Grand Canyon

In the last 40 years many books and articles have been published concerning the discoveries of ancient Egyptian hieroglyphs, coins, statues, mummies, art and ruins in North and South America. An ancient Egyptian pyramid and artifacts were reported in the Australian wilderness. Several ancient Egyptian artifacts were found in what is now the United States.

It is a fact that the ancient Egyptians built ocean going ships that were far larger than Columbus used on his journeys to America. Some of these Egyptian ships were described as more durable than any ships the early American explorers used. Ancient Egyptian ships traveled very rough and stormy seas in the Indian Ocean and cruised for thousands of miles. Ancient writings from over 2,000 years ago in the Middle East clearly prove ancient cultures knew of the round world. So why couldn't the Egyptians have sent expeditions to America?

It is a well-known fact that most of the knowledge and technology of the ancient world was lost when invaders burned the ten biggest libraries of antiquity. Could the records of ancient voyages to America have been lost when the great Egyptian library at Alexandria was burned?

There are reports of the remains of an ancient Egyptian ship found in water off the East Coast. An ancient Egyptian statue was found in Illinois.

The respected newspaper **Arizona Gazette** published an amazing Egyptian discovery in The Grand Canyon. The fact that this expedition was from the prestigious Smithsonian Institute rules out a hoax. The article appeared on April 5, 1909.

This news article reported that the institute's Professor S.A. Jordan was in charge of this expedition. The group was led by G.E. Kincaid who had been the first to discover the artifacts and returned with twelve Smithsonian professionals to verify the evidence. The discovery was located in a large, underground cavern high above the Colorado River. A cave opening led to long, stone, carved passageways that came to an underground community over 1,400 feet below. Kincaid was making explorations of the river and canyon for the Smithsonian Institute.

The newspaper account said the expedition followed Kincaid into the long passageway. The scientists carried bright electric lamps and found the passageway in a huge chamber. Several hallways led to dozens of smaller rooms. Corridors designed like spokes in a wheel radiated from a central location. Most of the hallways had dimensions up to 9 to 12 feet with walls up to a half foot thick. Passageways were hundreds of feet long. Their doorways were oval-shaped and ventilated by perfectly circular holes cut into the half foot thick walls. A major discovery was the mathematical precision of hewn and carved architecture. Walls were covered with hieroglyphs.

Artifact included vases, cups, bracelets, chisels, headgear, hammers, swords, axes, breastplates, shields, idols, statues and other items. Objects were manufactured in gold and copper with a precision more advanced than Native Indians in North America. This technology was said to have been unknown in the days of Columbus and the Middle Ages. The manufacturing technique was known to the ancient Egyptians and regarded a lost science.

A very remarkable discovery was a statue of a man with distinctly Asian features. How did this artifact get in a temple in the Grand Canyon? However, the mummified bodies reminded explorers of

Egyptian culture. Some of the artifacts were described as resembling ancient culture from the Nile Valley.

Many areas around the Grand Canyon mysteriously have Egyptian names like Horus Temple, Tower of Ra, Cheops Pyramid, Tower of Set, Osiris and Isis, etc. Marble masonry unknown to Native Indian cultures was found in the cavern.

For many more details good sources buy David Hatcher Childress' book *Lost Cities and Ancient Civilizations of North America* and Frank Joseph's *Unearthing Ancient America*. Both of these world explorers are famous for their remarkable and extensive research.

Unfortunately, further explorations were stopped because this discovery is on government land with trespassing penalties. Researchers learned that something was discovered that was so profound there is a government cover-up. No one is allowed into this area. Perhaps there are artifacts of priceless value.

The fact that an underground Egyptian Temple exists in the Grand Canyon is phenomenal because this discovery proves that ancient Egyptians navigated in boats across the vast ocean from Egypt to America. The ancient Egyptians were world explorers and navigators who explored many places in the world.

SIXTY-TWO

Indigo Boy Describes Mars

Many astronomers and NASA scientists theorize that Mars had oceans, rivers, vegetation and an atmosphere more like Earth billions of years ago. Space probe photos show evidence of ancient Martian rivers, oceans and what looks like forests of hardened trees. Richard Hoagland has acquired spectacular, censored photos that were "leaked out" of NASA files showing ancient ruins on Mars that appear to have been destroyed by a huge cataclysm. These photos include a small pyramid, sphinx, machinery, walls and what looks like ruined cities. Other photos from additional NASA sources show what looks like ancient straight roads with perfect configurations, buildings and what may be an ancient spaceport. Hoagland's startling book **Dark Mission, The Secret History of NASA** and David Hatcher Childress' book **Extraterrestrial Archaeology** clearly show these objects in official NASA photographs.

The famous author, explorer and archaeologist Zecharia Sitchen has published books stating that he translated ancient, Sumerian writings about Mars. Sitchen concluded that a planet between Mars and Jupiter exploded and ruined the Martian atmosphere and civilization with a massive meteor bombardment. Zecharia stated that survivors fled to Earth and colonized our planet in ancient times. Several theosophical and metaphysical books, as well as ancient Vedic texts, claim that most of those who died in Martian cataclysms reincarnated on the Earth.

It is remarkable how a seven year old boy named Boriska described details and facts about Mars at such a young age. However, the child genius began to tell stories about ancient megalithic cities, Martian spaceships and the Lost Continent of Lemuria that sounded far too sophisticated for a seven year old! The boy claimed he had fully-conscious recall of various past lives. Note that this memory was not the usual past life review obtained from hypnosis. This kid could vividly remember events that included a claimed past life on Mars while fully awake.

This narrative included an account of a planetary cataclysm on ancient Mars that destroyed its civilization and atmosphere. Some survivors fled to underground cities. Boriska said he flew to Earth in a spaceship and visited Lemuria which was also destroyed in a huge cataclysm. When Boriska made those comments the photos of the ruins of Martian cities, technology, the sphinx and pyramid had not yet been released to the public. Boriska also told of ancient wars involving Mars that sounded much like events that Zecharia Sitchin reported he translated in ancient tablets from the Middle East. The boy's details on the destruction of Lemuria matched those found in ancient texts from India like the Book of Dzyan---as well as ancient tablets from Burma that Colonel James Churchward wrote he translated. Linguists who have translated ancient Mayan writings also claim these same details of huge volcanic eruptions, exploding mountains, earthquakes and tidal wave submerging the land. The child claimed there were giant humans who lived in Lemuria. This information was in ancient Vedic texts from temples in India. How could a child know this data?

Boriska's parents verified that he picked up this information from his mind instead of reading about Lemuria, UFOs and Mars. The boy discussed metaphysics and astronomy at the age of two. By age seven Boriska was using advanced terminology.

Boriska has been described as an Indigo Child. These kids have amazing and rapid brain development, psychic abilities and far higher than average I.Q. scores. Boriska could read newspaper type at age one and a half, became an artist when he was two and could speak foreign languages as a child.

Several other famous metaphysical researchers like David Wilcock, Carla Rueckert (The Ra Material) and others claim that Boriska's version of ancient Mars and Lemuria is basically true. They also speak of millions of Martians dying and reincarnating on Earth. Other famous past-life hypnotherapists like Dr. Michael Newton, Dolores Cannon and Ruth Montgomery claim many of their clients had past lives on other planets. There are dozens of taped past-life memory recalls of these interplanetary lives.

Boriska was also able to describe details of interplanetary spaceship construction and propulsion that seemed impossible for such a young kid. The Russian Academy of Science was very impressed with Boriska's abilities.

The fact that indigo children are being born on Earth in our present generation is remarkable. They are mentally and spiritually more advanced and aware of inner truths. These indigo children may be able to make a difference in helping others on Earth.

Nonfiction

SIXTY-THREE

Elderly Years

Our elderly years are just as important as our earlier stages of life. We still have the opportunity to learn many things because of meaningful experiences in our daily lives. We should try to maintain a youthful attitude and an open mind.

An eager mind is a mind which continues to develop and grow. To acquire an observant awareness helps us become more alert. We can find out a lot about life. We should try to maintain a healthy outlook about life. Positive thoughts help us develop a higher consciousness. With a higher consciousness we can develop self realization in order to become illumined.

During one's senior years there is more time to enjoy hobbies and interests as well as to attend social groups and clubs. There is time to take walks and to read extensively. Gardening is a worthwhile hobby. Enjoying the sunshine and fresh air is important.

Elderly years is a time to reflect and recall special times in our lives. We should become close to God and become One with all life. We have the opportunity to travel to different places to appreciate scenery, people, cultural events and community activities.

Each stage of our lives is a time to awaken to worthwhile experiences. We can develop wisdom and maturity as we grow older. So, take advantage of your elderly years so you can have a full life.

Cecelia Frances Page

Nonfiction

SIXTY-FOUR

Knowledge About Antarctica

Antarctica is in the Southern Hemisphere at the South Pole. Antarctica is larger than Europe or Australia. But, it has no permanent population. This is because it is bitterly cold and mostly covered by a huge ice sheet, up to about 15,700 feet thick.

Antarctica is about 5,400,000 square miles. The highest point is Vinson Massif (16,864 feet). Scientists visit the South Pole and other parts of Antarctica to carry out research. They drill deep into the ice to collect samples. By counting the layers and identifying chemicals in them, they can see what weather and environmental conditions were like thousands of years ago.

Mount Erebus is an active volcano which overlooks Ross Sea in Antarctica. Antarctica is the coldest continent. The world's lowest air temperature of -89.2C (-128.6F) was recorded at Vostok scientific station in 1983.

Elephant seals live in the waters around Antarctica and southern South America. These lumbering mammals, also called sea elephants, weigh up to 3,600 kg. (8,000 lb.). Among the sea mammals, only whales are larger. Penguins are native to Antarctica. These flightless birds are excellent swimmers and they feed in the oceans around the continent. Four species of penguins breed on Antarctica. Others breed on the islands north of Antarctica.

Antarctica was the last continent to be explored. Captain James Cook, from Britain, explored the southern oceans in the 18th Century. He crossed the Antarctic Circle but did not sight land. The first men were probably seal and whale hunters to stop on the continent in the early 19th Century.

American, French and British expeditions charted parts of the coast around 1840. James Clark Ross made an important expedition to the Ross Sea. He discovered two volcanoes that he named Erebus and Terror. These were the names of his ships.

In 1911, two men reached the South Pole. Roald Amendsen from Norway reached the South Pole by December 14, 1911. The British explorer Robert Falcon Scott reached the Pole just over a month later. However, all the members of his expedition died on the return trip. Roald Amundsen was the first man to reach the South Pole. The U.S. Amundsen-Scott Station at the Pole is named after him and his British adversary Robert Falcon Scott, who also reached the Pole died on the way home.

Scientific stations operate throughout the year in Antarctica. They study such things as the continents' geology, its mineral resources and the climate.

Antarctica has resources even if it is cold. Coal has been found on this continent. Deposits of minerals are chromium, copper, gold, iron, lead, manganese, platinum, silver, tin, titanium, uranium and zinc. Seven countries have claimed parts of Antarctica so they can exploit its resources.

Nations with an interest in Antarctica have signed treaties concerning this continent. The Antarctic Treaty of 1959 states that the continent must be used only for peaceful purposes. It forbids the testing of nuclear weapons and the dumping of nuclear wastes. In 1991, it was also agreed that the exploitation of minerals should be banned for 50 years. This agreement came into existence in 1998.

Many people believe that Antarctica, the last true wilderness on Earth, should be protected. Scientists from many nations have called on governments to make Antarctica a World Park controlled by the United Nations. The establishment of a World Park would protect Antarctica and its wildlife, including the creatures that live in the seas around it. Tourism would be permitted but controlled to protect this continent.

In winter the ice shelves extend to form floating packs of ice that stretches 1,000 miles from the coast. In summer the ice breaks up to form flat icebergs or ice floes. Recently, huge icebergs the size of a small country have broken free. Scientists think this may be caused by global warming, which may be melting the ice shelves around the continent and causing an increase in snowfall. The partial melting of the Antarctic ice sheet could raise sea levels around the world by between 5 and 20M (16 to 66 feet), submerging many islands and coastal areas.

In the mid-1980s, scientists in Antarctica discovered that the ozone layer over Antarctica was being thinned by pollution, creating an "ozone hole." By 1998, the "hole" covered an area about three times as large as the United States. The ozone layer, between 12 and 24 km. (7.5 to 15 miles) above the Earth, protects the land from the sun's harmful ultraviolet rays, which can cause skin cancer and damage to crops. Many nations now ban the use of the chemicals that are causing the damage.

Antarctica has many underground lakes and hundreds of pools of water. Lambert Glacier is located at Amery Ice Shelf. The Antarctica Islands above Antarctica are the Falkland Islands, South Georgia (UK), South Shetland Islands (UK), South Orkney Islands (UK) and South Sandwich Islands (UK). There are East Antarctica and West Antarctica. The South Pole is in the center of Antarctica.

One of the most spectacular and amazing discoveries in Antarctica is unknown to most of the public. This event leaked out in some media in 2001 and was quickly covered-up by Britain and the United States.

An enormous freshwater lake far beneath the ice layer was discovered that was an incredible 300 miles long! This lake was about 50 miles wide and an amazing 2000 feet deep. There are relatively few lakes on the Earth's surface this large. Lake Vostok is bigger than many of the states in the USA and even some countries.

The ice layer over this lake is nearly a mile thick. The visibility was like at dawn on the surface. A dome of atmosphere over the ice is over a half mile high.

One of the most remarkable discoveries was that the water was averaging 50 degrees underneath the freezing ice instead of a more expected 33 degrees. Some areas of the lake were up to 65 degrees! That water temperature is found at many Southern California beaches in early summer. Geothermal hot spots were speculated to exist in these zones. It was theorized that this zone has been so sealed off from the surface that it could contain prehistoric life! There are no publicized surface entrances into this pristine environment, according to some researchers. Furthermore, a mysterious magnetic anomaly was detected at the north end of the lake.

Although ten years has passed there have been no further press releases available concerning the results of official plans to explore this lake. The discovery was by a Cambridge University team from London backed by NASA technology.

Another mystery concerns two women who were attempting to ski across Antarctica around that time. U.S. Navy Special Forces reportedly forced these skiers to stop the completion of their trip and removed them by aircraft against their will. The women reported something "unusual" they had seen. Much of the data on this lake was published in Australia's popular NEXUS magazine. Many people wondered what was secretly going on under the huge lake.

Perhaps a clue is another mysterious report from Antarctica in 1947. Admiral Byrd was the most famous Antarctic explorer, and his associate Commander Bunger was sent to explore uncharted regions of the ice. This report states that Bunger's flight discovered an amazing "green oasis" of dense, green forests and small lakes in the middle of ice that stretched to the horizon in all directions! Bunger's seaplane was said to have landed on one of these small unfrozen lakes. His crew was startled to find patches of water temperatures in the mid-sixties and air temperatures well above freezing! The verdant valley was surrounded by ice cliffs thousands of feet high. The crew allegedly saw a large animal in the valley. This discovery was soon reported in various newspapers and magazines for one day only. The information stated there would be further investigations. Yet, there were no further news releases.

Over 40 years later the "lost diary" of Admiral Byrd was circulated. This record was allegedly released by one of Admiral Byrd's relatives after his death. The diary stated that the admiral had also explored this oases and found an opening into a huge cavernous area underground that was inhabited by people who did not want outsiders invading. In addition to this diary, researchers like Michael Barton and Raymond Bernard wrote that they had uncovered details on these findings by Admiral Byrd as long ago as the 1950s. There have been others who confessed they witnessed evidence of this discovery. Byrd reportedly attempted to have this information published in National Geographic but it was blocked due to National Security. It was reported that this was regarded as a strategic zone that the Pentagon wanted to gain sovereignty over and a very favorable location for a base.

Nonfiction

SIXTY-FIVE

Do Dinosaurs Live Today?

Most traditional historians believe dinosaurs became extinct about 65 million years ago. However, ancient cave wall paintings and rock carvings from Peru and Mexico show living dinosaurs surrounded by men. Some of this art shows humans fighting huge dinosaurs. The creatures appear to be authentic replications. How did these men from only a few thousands years ago know what these dinosaurs looked like? There are no known fossil remains in those areas to copy.

In the last century explorers have reported finding native tribes deep in the rainforests of Africa and Brazil who told of living dinosaur sightings. These natives fear these creatures and are very serious and explicit. There are numerous witnesses who have seen dinosaurs.

The late John Keel published some excellent research on sightings all over the world of what appear to be prehistoric animals. Flying dinosaur birds have been reported by numerous Indian tribes, cowboys and settlers in the U.S. desert southwest for centuries. Did a small fraction of the dinosaurs survive and procreate? After all, crocodiles, iguanas and cockroaches survived the famous mass-extinction of dinosaurs.

Well-known, documented and multi-witness sightings of The Loch Ness Monster and the Lake Champlain Monster span the decades. Photographs of these huge creatures show an animal that has an extremely long neck, small head and body very similar to one of the most famous dinosaurs. Could that creature have survived underwater during a cataclysm?

However, the best evidence for present dinosaurs is from deep in the wilderness of Northern Australia. Many reports with many witnesses have come from Queensland, the Outback and Northern Territories for the last century. Native aborigines and white settlers, explorers, hunters and miners have reported such dinosaur encounters. Footprints that look just like dinosaur feet have been examined. Smashed bushes and trees have been examined after loud trampling was heard. Some cases involve multiple witnesses. There have been too many witnesses to deny.

The most common sightings describe a Tyrannosaurus-like animal at least 20 feet tall! One tribe of aborigines reported one of these dinosaurs entered their camp near Ayers Rock and they drove it off with spears. Smaller dinosaurs were also reported.

In the 1890s cattlemen in the extreme northern gulf country reported one of these beasts was so big it was carrying away their cattle for food. Around Mount Surprise there is a rock carving of a dinosaur. Reptilian footprints about one and a half feet long were found in the wilderness.

Early colonists in Australia in the 1700s were told detailed descriptions of extinct dinosaurs by aborigine tribes. These accounts were over a hundred years before anthropologists figured out what these dinosaurs even looked like! If the natives hadn't seen these remains and drawings of what they looked like, how can we explain their accurate descriptions of the beasts they witnessed? Aborigines had no access to these remains.

For more details on sightings of prehistoric animals good reading material is found in many issues of **Fate** magazine, as well as the books by John Keel, David Hatcher Childress and **The Search for Australia's Unknown Animals** by Rex and Heather Gilroy. All of these sources are highly recommended and well researched. The famous author of Earth's most amazing mysteries was Charles Fort.

This meticulous researcher documented many accounts of sightings of monstrous creatures.

If a lizard, snake and centipede can survive for 65 million years, then why couldn't a dinosaur? There have simply been far too many sightings of dinosaurs, for too many decades to ignore.

Nonfiction

SIXTY-SIX

Hemp Could Help Humanity

Hemp has proven to be one of the most useful crops in the history of humanity. In ancient, medieval and Renaissance centuries this stalk and fiber was used to make durable clothing, feed millions of people, manufacture superior rope, build roofing and walls and make sails for ships. George Washington and some other American leaders grew hemp plantations. During wars hemp was useful in nations that ran out of cotton, wool, silk, leather, paper, fuel and many other necessities. For centuries hemp was considered as important as cotton, wood, animal skins and wool.

In modern nations that use hemp as a major crop tens of thousands of jobs were created, and taxes on this product have created billions of dollars to help damaged economies. If the United States created a massive hemp industry it could generate billions of dollars toward schools, health care, poverty programs and other valuable programs that are greatly suffering from budget cuts. Furthermore, it would generate millions of jobs in farming, manufacturing and distribution that would greatly alleviate the unemployment crisis.

Large hemp crops could feed the hungry, starving and undernourished people of the world. Hemp seeds provide complete protein and all of the essential amino acids. Hemp is an excellent, natural source of the B-Complex vitamins, iron, zinc, omega 3 and

6, calcium, Vitamin C, Vitamin D, Vitamin E, beta carotene, anti-oxidants, magnesium and other vital nutrients. Hemp contains far more nutrients than wheat, oat, corn, barley, rice and nuts. There are very few foods with so many nutrients and essential fatty acids. This plant and its seeds have far more nutrients than wheat, corn, rice, barley or oats. Hemp is a natural food that is best grown organically. This plant can be grown faster than most crops. The result is that hemp is a superior crop to feed the poor in Third World nations.

Hemp bark also has the longest and most durable fiber of all plants. The plant is used for fiberboard, roofing, flooring, wall board, caulking, cement, paint, paneling, particleboard, plaster, plywood, reinforced concrete, insulation, pipes, bricks and biodegradable plastic composites which are tougher than steel. A major advantage is that this form of manufacturing greatly reduces the need for oil that pollutes the environment, causes wars, is more expensive to produce and is a diminishing resource. Hemp seed oil is a much better alternative.

Hemp is a natural product that does not need pesticides which damage the soil, wildlife and the human body. Hemp residues actually improve the soil as a superior form of compost. Instead of polluting the atmosphere, hemp has properties that reduce damaging carbon in the air.

Hemp is an excellent product to make paper and cardboard. So, mass-production would eliminate the disaster of destroying the world's forests for wood to manufacture paper products.

The reader may want to know why hemp isn't a major crop in the United States and other nations. The answer is that the plant looks much like marijuana and is related to that species of plants. However, it is impossible to get stoned on industrial hemp plants. These hemp seeds do not contain the drug THC found in marijuana.

Small traces of THC found in certain hemp varieties are easily eliminated in the industrial variety and as a food.

Furthermore, can you imagine somebody trying to smoke clothing made out of hemp and lighting up their construction materials, rope, bricks, flooring, roofing, plaster and plywood to get "high?" Even if these silly antics occurred the smokers would simply not get stoned.

The founding President of the United States and Father of Democracy grew a lot of hemp. If hemp was good enough for those men it is certainly good for America today.

Essential fatty acids are necessary for good health and are responsible for the luster in our skin, hair and eyes and even the clarity in our thought processes, as they oxygenate every cell in our body. They also lubricate and clear the arteries, strengthen immunity and help prevent viral and other threats to the immune system. However, EFAs are not produced by the human body. they must be obtained from food sources.

Hempseed oil can be frozen for a longer period of time than other oils without risking container breakage. Due to its highly unsaturated fatty acid chains, it does not go solid. Furthermore, high-quality oils that are stored properly don't need any added preservatives (anti-oxidants).

Nonfiction

SIXTY-SEVEN

South America, Land of Opportunity

South America, the fourth-largest continent, covers over 12 percent of the world's longest mountain range and the world's largest rainforest. The countries of South America contain rich farmland and many other resources. However, they are far less developed than Canada and the United States.

Argentina, Brazil, Chile and Venezuela are the most prosperous countries. Seven independent countries are classified as lower Middle-income countries and Guyana is the poorest South American country. South America's population includes Native Americans (Amerindians) and people of European and black African origin. Many people are mixed descent.

Simon Bolivar (1783-1830) was a South American military leader. His victories won independence for Bolivia, Columbia, Ecuador, Peru and Venezuela. Spain and Portugal ruled much of South America between the 16th and early 19th centuries.

South America is 6,885,000 square miles. There are 12 independent countries. The population in South America is 323,924,000. There are Andean condors, llamas and a variety of butterflies.

VENEZUELA

Venezuela faces the Caribbean Sea, which is part of the Atlantic Ocean. Christopher Columbus landed on the coast of Venezuela in 1498. Venezuela declared itself independent of Spain in 1811. Venezuela is one of the world's top producers of oil, which has helped it to develop its economy. Venezuela is one of the most prosperous countries in South America. Some Venezuelans are rich and many live in poverty. Caracas, Venezuela's capital, founded in 1567, was the birth place of the South American hero Simon Bolivar. Caracas is a modern city which is 7 miles from its port, La Guaira, on the coast.

Gold and diamonds are mined in Venezuela, together with coal bauxite (aluminum ore), iron ore, gypsum and phosphate rock, which is used to make fertilizers. But oil and oil products make up three-quarters of the country's exports.

Roraima is the highest peak of the Guiana Highlands. It reaches 9,904 feet at the point where the borders of Venezuela, Guyana, and Brazil meet. Several rivers rise in these highlands.

Tourism is a growing industry. Venezuela has many beautiful beaches along the dry, warm Caribbean Coast. Margarita is an offshore island which is known for its pearls. About 600,000 tourists visit Venezuela every year.

Guyana (formerly British Guyana), Suriname (formerly Dutch Guiana), and French Guyana, a French overseas department, are situated in northeastern South America. Together, they are called "Guyanas". They have narrow coastal plains where most of the people live with plateaus and mountains inland. Guyana is a poor country, but Suriname is more prosperous because of its bauxite deposits. French Guiana depends largely on financial and administrative support from France.

The capital of Guyana is Georgetown. The capital of Suriname is Paramaribo. The capital of French Guyana is Cayenne. The total population of Guyana is 839,000 people. The total population in Suriname is 432,000 people. The total population in French Guiana is 153,000 people. The official language is English in Guyana. In

Suriname the official language is French. Christianity is the major religion in Guyana, Suriname and French Guiana.

Hardwoods are important products in the Guyanas. Rainforests containing valuable trees, such as greenheart, cover 90 percent of French Guiana and Suriname and 85 percent of Guyana. The timber industry produces logs and plywood. Bauxite is the ore from which the metal aluminum is made. Bauxite and aluminum make up more than 70 percent of the exports of Suriname. Guyana also exports bauxite. French Guiana also exports bauxite. French Guyana has some bauxite deposits, but they are largely undeveloped.

Kourou, northwest of Cayenne, the capital of French Guiana, has been the rocket-launching site of the European Space Agency since 1968. France earns money by launching the satellites of other countries. Sugarcane is one of the main crops of the Guyanas. It makes up about one-quarter of the exports of Guyana. The other major crop is rice, which is grown on about three-quarters of the farmland in Suriname. Fishing is another important industry.

Georgetown, the capital of Guyana, is built on low coastal land. Strong sea walls and drainage canals prevent flooding of the coastal plain. Only about one-third of the Guyanese live in towns. The rest are farmers.

BRAZIL

Brazil is the fifth largest country in the world. Only Russia, Canada, China and the United States are bigger. This country's main regions are the Amazon Basin, the dry northeast, where farmers rear cattle and the southeast, Brazil's most thickly populated region. Until 1822 the country was a Portuguese colony. Today Brazil is a rapidly developing country. However, many Brazilians are poor. 23 percent of the people work on farms. Brazil is one of the world's leading producers of crops and livestock.

Sao Paulo, Rio de Janeiro and Salvador are the largest cities in Brazil. The capital of Brazil is Brasilia. The Amazon River is the world's second longest river after the Nile. The Amazon had more water than any other river. The Amazon Basin contains the world's largest rainforest. In recent years about one-tenth of the forest has been destroyed. Plants and animals are vanishing before scientists have had a chance to study them.

Sloths are strange hairy mammals that live in the forests. They use their hook-like-claws to hang upside down from branches. They rarely move except to reach more of the leaves which they eat. They remain so still that lichens and mosses grow on their fur.

Sugar Loaf Mountain is a landmark of Rio de Janeiro, Brazil's second largest city. This city has magnificent scenery and is famous for its beaches, nightlife and colorful carnivals. Native Americans live in decreasing numbers in the vast rainforests of the Amazon Basin. Many have given up their traditional way of life and now work in mines. The future of these people is threatened because their forest home is being destroyed. Some groups have already died out.

Cars, aircraft, chemicals, processed food, iron and steel, paper and textiles are leading industries in Brazil. This country's rich mineral reserves include bauxite, chrome, diamonds, gold, iron ore, manganese and tin.

COLUMBIA

Columbia, in the northwest corner of the continent, is South America's fourth-largest country. In the north, it faces the Caribbean Sea, an arm of the Atlantic Ocean. The Pacific Ocean lies to the west. Columbia has three main regions, including the northern part of the Andes Mountains. Coastal plains lie to the north and west. The southeast contains forested plains, which are drained by tributaries of the Orinoco and Amazon rivers.

The country was the heart of the Spanish colony of New Granada, which also included Venezuela, Ecuador and Panama in Central America. It achieved independence in 1819. The total population in Columbia is 37,541,000 people. The capital city is Bogota. The official language is Spanish.

Statues and other carvings were made by the Chibcha people, who founded a major civilization in the Andes region. Spanish invaders conquered the Chibcha between 1536 and 1538. Spain introduced Roman Catholicism and ruled the country until 1819, when Simon Bolivar's army defeated Spanish forces in a battle. Bogota, capital of Columbia, stands on a high plateau surrounded by mountains in the eastern Andes. The Spanish conquerors of the Chibcha founded the city in 1538. The Andes region is the home of about three-quarters of the population of Columbia.

Coffee is Columbia's leading export crop. Other exports include oil, chemicals, wood and fish products, textiles and coal. 27 percent of the people are employed in agriculture. Cattle are raised and crops include bananas, cotton, rice and sugarcane. Coca is a native plant of Columbia. The leaves of some types of coca are used to make cocaine, a drug that is illegally exported to the United State and other countries.

Emeralds were once traded by the Chibcha people. Today, Columbia produces about four-fifths of the world's emeralds. Columbia also produces coal, gold, oil and natural gas and salt, which is used in the country's large chemical industry.

Jaguars once lived all over South America. They are found in isolated areas of forests and in national parks. They are the largest of the wild cats found in the Americas. Over-hunting and destruction of forests threaten their survival.

ECUADOR

Ecuador lies on the equator. Ecuador is a Spanish name which means equator. Ecuador's main regions are the hot coastal lowlands, the Andes Mountains and the humid eastern plains, which are drained by the Amazon and its tributaries.

The Incas conquered the region of Ecuador in the 15th Century. The Spanish defeated the Incas in 1534. Ecuador became independent in 1822. The capital of Ecuador is Quito. The total population of this country is 11,698,000 as of 1999. The largest cities are Guayaquil and Cuenca. The official language is Spanish. 93% of the people are Roman Catholics.

Fishing is an important industry in the coastal waters. Herring, mackerel and shrimp are important seafood. Shrimp is formed in ponds. Bananas, coca and coffee are leading export crops. Forestry is also important. Ecuador is the largest world producer of balsa wood. Mining is a major industry. Ecuador's leading exports are oil and oil products.

Three ranges of the Andes Mountains form the backbone of Ecuador. Between the ranges are high plateaus or basins. Nearly half of the country's people live on these high plateaus. The mild climate is pleasant.

Cotopaxi, south of the city, Quito, is one of the world's highest active volcanoes at 19,347 feet. When it erupted in 1877, avalanches of mud, caused by melting snow-mixing with volcanic ash, buried large areas. Around 1,000 people were killed. Ecuador has more than 30 active volcanoes.

PERU

Peru contains active volcanoes in a valley of the Andes Mountains in high plateaus between the ranges. East of the Andes are plains covered by rainforests. The Miraflores district of the capital city of Lima looks a lot like Santa Monica, California in its beach cliffs, beaches, ocean, vegetation, architecture and frequent fog and clouds. Downtown Lima looks a lot like downtown Los Angeles.

Over 90% of Peru's coastline is barren deserts that are usually cool rather than hot. The frequent cool foggy or cloudy weather and chilly ocean is remarkable for coastline closer to the equator than Hawaii or Tahiti and far into the tropics. Barren hills and deserts behind the beach instead of jungles are evident. The reason is that these beaches are bordered by the cold ocean current from Antarctica. This current moves away from the coast at the extreme northwestern tip of Peru where there is a very small zone of warm weather, water and tropical vegetation near the Ecuador border.

From about A.D. 1200 Peru was the heart of the great Inca civilization. Spanish soldiers conquered the Incas in 1533. Peru became independent from Spain in 1821.

Native Americans now make up nearly half of the population. The Inca language, Quechua, is one of Peru's two official languages.

Larger cities are Arequipa and Callao. The total population is 24,288,000.

Archaeologists have explored Peru. Caral is an ancient city that was estimated over 5,000 years old. It has incredible temples, pyramids, paved roads, plazas, aqueducts, and buildings. Its architecture is far more advanced than the Incas who arrived thousands of years later. It is the only city ever discovered by archaeologists that had a truly Golden Age. There was no evidence of a military force, weapons, war or violence!

Machu Picchu, an ancient Inca city, stands on a peak in south central Peru. The Incas ruled one of the largest Native American empires. At its height, the empire stretched from southern Columbia, through Ecuador and Peru, into Chile and Argentina. Archaeologists in recent times have discovered that Machu Picchu was originally created by a more advanced and ancient civilization than Incan, with far different architecture and masonry. Engineering using the more primitive style of the Incas was built on top of the older structures. The Incas never told the conquering Spaniards about Machu Picchu which was not even discovered until the 20th Century. Remains indicated the city was mostly inhabited by women. The site is so remote there are no roads and access was by the famous Inca trail. More recently an old-style railroad was built tunneling through the high mountains to the little Indian village of Agua Caliente. A narrow road winds up the nearby mountain to Machu Picchu where there are no hotels, restaurants or tourist shops. Accommodations in the village are very primitive. However, there is a great Indian market place for bargain shopping and once excellent restaurant.

Toucans are tropical birds of Central and South America. There are many kinds with large, brightly colored bills. Some are found in Peru's eastern forests where they gather in small flocks high in the trees.

The desert floor at Nazca in southern Peru has large patterns and drawings of animals and birds. Some are 1.2 miles long and completely visible only from the air. On the ground it is impossible to see this art or the straight lines carved in the ground for dozens of miles in perfect patterns. These lines go through deserts, canyons and up hills perfectly straight. Nobody knows the significance of these ancient markings or who made them. Archaeologists theorize they may have a religious or astronomical purpose.

The mighty Amazon River rises in the Peruvian Andes in a small stream called the Apurimac. The Apurimac eventually flows into the Ucayali River, which flows north to join the Maranon River. From here the Amazon flows east to the Atlantic Ocean.

Lake Titicaca, the world's highest navigable lake, lies on Peru's border with Bolivia. It occupies a basin between ranges of the Andes Mountains, at 12,507 feet above sea level. Local people use reed boats to sail on the lake. Many Indians live on floating homes made out of reeds.

Cuzco was the capital city of the Incas. Cuzco looks very ancient with cobblestone streets, Inca architecture and Spanish buildings and cathedrals dating from the 1500s-1600s. Much of the city looks like the 16th Century. There are thousands of Indians dressed in their colorful, traditional, historical costumes. Cuzco is over 12,000 feet in the Andes. The air is so thin many tourists find breathing difficult. Cozy hotels with the 19th century look are as low as $20 a night. Delicious restaurant and store food sells for a fraction of U.S. and European prices. Near the city is the legendary "Sacred Valley of the Incas" where spectacular ancient ruins and Indian lifestyles are viewed.

Not all of the Indians are Incas. There are Quechuas and Aymaras living in primitive conditions like their ancestors. They speak native languages. It was amazing when the invading Spanish armies found that much of the royalty and leaders of the ancient Incas had blonde or red hair and some had blue eyes and light skin. The majority of the Incas were dark-skinned and haired. They were amazed to find some Christian artifacts in Incan temples and objects and words that were traced to Britain and Europe! Perhaps there were secret or lost voyages to South America before Columbus. The Spanish invaders also found statues and carvings of Europeans, Asians and Middle Easterns in the Andes!

BOLIVIA

Bolivia contains part of the Andes Mountains together with forested plains in the north and east. Native Americans have lived in the area for over 10,000 years. The main groups today are the Aymara and the Quechua. Bolivian culture, like that of much of South America, is a mix of local and European influences. The capital of Bolivia is La Paz. The total population in Bolivia is 7,588,000 people in 1909. The largest cities are La Paz and Santa Cruz. The official languages are Spanish, Aymara and Quechua. 89% of the people are Roman Catholics.

Tin is used in Bolivia, a country rich in minerals, including oil, gold and silver. Bolivia exports minerals. However, it has few manufacturing industries. Soya beans and timber are also exported. Potatoes and wheat are grown on the Altiplano, a plateau between the eastern and western ranges of the Andes. Bananas, coca, coffee and maize are grown at lower, warmer levels. 47% of the people work in agriculture.

Reed pipes and flutes are played by Native American musicians in the Andes. Their unusual music is played at traditional festivals. Traditional dress is still worn by many of the poorer people in the mountains. The women wear bright skirts and bowler hats.

Antonio Jose de Sucre (1795-1830) helped to end Spanish rule in South America. Sucre, the official capital of Bolivia, is named after the great general. This city, which was founded in 1538, contains Bolivia's Supreme Court; but most government buildings are in La Paz, the actual capital and largest city.

The major tourist attraction in Bolivia is Lake Titicaca and is centered at Copacabana. This is an extremely popular boating and hiking town. Offshore is the legendary Island of the Sun where the famous Incan Temple of the Sun was located and where the Incan civilization began. Offshore divers found a stone temple 60 to 100 feet underwater, a long wall, vases underwater passageways and other ruins of a prehistoric city that sank in an immense cataclysm. This city existed many thousands of years *before* the Incas! It was built by an unrecorded "lost race." Some explorers call this site *"the*

South American Atlantis." Nearby Indians live in floating homes made of reeds.

Bolivia also contains the ruins of the *"oldest city" ever discovered* on the surface of Earth and the most advanced engineering of any ruins on the surface of the Earth! Archaeologists state that the Spanish and Incas never had the tools and engineering to build this complex. Furthermore, the Incas originated about 800 years ago. Archaeologists and researchers who did the most thorough scientific research at Tijuanaco concluded it was built up to 17,000 years ago! That date is amazing since most historians date the oldest ruins in Egypt and Sumer about 4,500 years ago (where scholars used to believe civilization first began). Yet, they do not know who built this city.

Explorers in the 1970s said there was no machinery that could lift and transport these stone blocks. Historians marveled at how the Egyptians could lift 3 to 20 ton stones at the pyramids. Yet, stones weighing up to 500 to 1,000 tons were lifted to build Tijuanano-Puma Punku, and transported over rough terrain and canyons from a quarry on the horizon. Modern drills and power saws would break trying to cut and shape these stones harder than metal. . Yet, the blocks are perfectly fit so smooth and tight, with no cement, that a credit card cannot be inserted between them. Many stone blocks are engineered with amazing mathematical precision like in modern buildings. Nearby is ruins of a seaport and canals but there is no water to the horizons. An immense cataclysm destroyed this culture. Some historians and archaeologists believe this site was part of the Atlantean or Lemurian empires. For many more details read my book REMARKABLE WORLD TRAVELS.

PARAGUAY

Rivers make up most of Paraguay's boundaries. This land consists mostly of large plains, plateaus and hills. The climate is warm and humid. Most people live in the east. The Guaranis were the first or earliest—known people of Paraguay. The Guarani language is now one of the country's two official languages. Most of the people in

Paraguay are mestizos of mixed Native American and European origins. The capital city is Asuncion. The largest cities are Asuncion and San Lorenzo. The total population in 1999 was 4,955,000 people. The official languages are Spanish and Guarani. 85% of the people are Roman Catholics.

Gauchos are cowboys who work on ranches in Paraguay and elsewhere on the grassy plains called pampas. Half of the people work in farming. Soya beans, cotton, oilseed cakes, vegetable oils, meat and hides are leading exports.

Hydroelectric power stations provide Paraguay with abundant electricity. Paraguay shores the huge Itaipu Dam with Brazil. When it was completed in 1991, this dam became one of the world's largest.

Quebracho trees grow in Paraguay and Argentina. Tannin, which is used for tanning hides, is extracted from quebracho wood. Forestry is important in Paraguay. However, this country has no major mineral deposits.

Asuncion, capital of Paraguay was founded by Spanish settlers in 1537 at the junction of the Paraguay and Pilcomayo rivers. Asuncion is the country's main industrial city. Manufactured products include cement, processed food, leather goods and textiles.

Soccer is Paraguay's most popular sport. Soccer is played throughout much of South America; especially in Argentina, Brazil and Uruguay, which have distinguished records in international soccer competition

Giant anteaters feed on the plentiful supplies of ants and termites found in the humid forests and plains. These animals tear open the anthills with their strong claws and lick up the ants. They have a long, sticky tongues.

CHILE

Chile is more than 10 times as long as it is wide. Its eastern borders run through the high Andes. Mountains to the west of the land descend through valleys and basins to the coastal plain along the Pacific Ocean. The Atacama Desert is in the North. The

Central Valley is in the center of Chile. The Central Valley has hot, dry summers and mild, rainy winters. This region contains three-quarters of the population. To the south, it gets colder and rainier. The far south is one of the world's stormiest places.

Mestizos are 75 percent of Chile's population. People of European descent are 20 percent. Native Americans make up only 3 percent of the population. Until 1818 most of the country was a colony of Spain.

The capital city is Santiago. The total population is 14,419,000 people in 1999. The official language is Spanish. 77% of the people are Roman Catholics.

Fishing is a major industry and Chile has one of the world's largest fishing fleets. The waters off the north coast are especially rich in anchovettas, mackerel and sardines. Grapes are grown in the warm Central Valley. Chile is an important producer of wines. 19 percent of the people work in agriculture. Major crops include beans, fruits, maize and wheat. Farmers also keep cattle, sheep and other animals.

Copper is the leading product in Northern Chile. Copper and other minerals make up about 40 percent of Chile's exports. Manufacturing is increasing and making Chile one of the most prosperous countries in South America.

Vicunas are wild relatives of the domestic llamas. Their silky fleece produces some of the finest wool in the world. The Incas prized the wool so highly that only their kings could wear it. Vicuna are endangered by hunting and are now protected.

Active volcanoes are found along the western side of the Andes Mountains. Many other peaks are extinct volcanoes. Eruptions and earthquakes are common because western South America lies on an unstable part of the Earth's crust.

ARGENTINA

Argentina is the second largest country in South America. The Andes Mountains lie in the West. In the center and north lie large plains, with the fertile pampas region called Patagonia. At the tip of Argentina lies the island of Tierra del Fuego, separated from the mainland by the Magellan Strait, which links the Atlantic and Pacific oceans. The weather is warmer and wet in the north and cold and dry in the south.

Argentina was part of a Spanish colony until 1816. About 85 percent of the people are of European descent. Mestizos make up most of the remaining 15 percent. Buenos Aires, capital of Argentina, was found by the Spanish in the 16th Century. It is now the country's chief industrial city. About 88% of Argentina's people live in cities and towns. The largest cities in Argentina are Buenos Aires, Cordoba and Rosario. The official language is Spanish. 91 percent of the people are Roman Catholics.

Iguacu Falls are magnificent falls which lie on the Iguacu River on the Argentina-Brazil border. These falls are about 2.2 miles wide and up to 269 feet high.

Cattle ranches are found in northern Argentina. Patagonia has large sheep farms. Farming is a major industry. Besides meat and wool, Argentina produces citrus fruits, cotton, grapes, maize, soya beans, sugarcane and tea.

Manufacturing has increased in Argentina in the last 50 years, making the country the most prosperous and developed in South America. Manufacturers include electrical equipment, printed materials, processed food and transportation equipment.

Aconcagua, an extinct volcano in the Andes close to the border with Chile, is the highest peak in North and South America. It reaches a height of 22,835 feet above sea level.

Tango dancing began in Argentina. The Argentine people consider it as their national dance. It shows Spanish influences. The tango became popular around the world in the early art of the 20th Century.

URUGUAY

Uruguay is South America's second smallest country, after Suriname. It is a land of grassy plains and hills. 90 percent of the people now live in cities and towns. Native Americans once occupied

Uruguay, but only a few Amerindians remain. This country was part of a Spanish colony until 1828. People of European descent make up 86 percent of the population. Mestizos are 8 percent and descendants of black Africans are 6 percent. The capital city is Montevideo. The larger cities are Montevideo, Salto and Paysand. The official language is Spanish. 78 percent of the people are Roman Catholics. Montevideo is the chief port and stands on the coast where the Rio de la Plata estuary meets the Atlantic Ocean. Montevideo was founded in 1726. Its suburbs contain most of Uruguay's industries.

Tourism is a leading activity in which it employs many people in the coastal resorts. About 90 percent of the people now live in cities and towns. About two million people visit Uruguay's sandy beaches every year. Tourists come mainly from Argentina.

Uruguay's arts are also greatly influenced by Spanish culture, through local themes, such as gaucho legends that are also popular. Gaucho rodeos attract many spectators, but soccer is the most popular sport. Uruguay has a fine record in international soccer competitions. Other parts include basketball and rugby. Textiles are among the leading manufacturers including beer, cement and processed food. Uruguay is one of the more prosperous of the developing countries in South America.

South America is a land of opportunities. You can enjoy learning about ancient Indians who lived there. There are scenic beaches, high Andes Mountains, beautiful rivers and some waterfalls. Part of South America is in the tropical zone. There is the driest desert in the world where it may not rain for over 20 years in parts. Parts of the Amazon are so remote and forested they have never even been explored. There are mysterious jungle tribes of white skinned Indians with blonde or red hair. There are interesting jungles and tropical forests, animals and interesting plants. You can enjoy touring through South America. There are glaciers, icebergs and penguins in the extreme south. South America has the highest mountain peaks in the Western Hemisphere. Very ancient, abandoned, mysterious and culturally advanced deserted cities exist in the dense Amazon jungle—where lost races unknown to historians once lived. A mysterious and lost civilization lies on the ocean bottom off the coast of Venezuela.

SIXTY-EIGHT

Anastasia's Garden Techniques

Anastasia lives in Russia on a deserted bank of the Siberian Ob River. She lives outdoors and she is close to nature in the woodlands. Anastasia is spiritually aware. She had learned to nurture seeds before planting them. Anastasia communicates to creatures and plants in a loving way. Anastasia planted seeds in garden plots such as raspberries, currants, gooseberries, cucumbers, tomatoes, wild strawberries and different apple trees. She grows healing herbs to heal the human body.

Vladimir Megre, a famous author from Russia, who interviewed Anastasia, said she told him, "The chief physician is your own body. Right from the start it was endowed with the ability to know which herb should be used and when. It is capable of warding off disease even before its outward manifestations. Nobody else can replace your body, for this is your personal physician, given individually to you by God and personal only to you."

Anastasia told Vladimir Megre that weeds are valuable in the garden because they maintain a life force. According to Anastasia, "When the seeds develop into plants and eventually produce fruit, these fruits can help prevent diseases." Anastasia believes that organic, healthy vegetables and fruit can sustain one's body. A person who eats only natural, organic foods should be much healthier.

Mikhair Nikolaevich Prokhorov, Director of ecological programming for a private firm in Moscow, with a doctoral degree in Biology, agrees with Anastasia. He stated, "The possibility is of the direct influence of human beings on the grown and development of plants and in certain situations on the health and behavior of animals."

The curing of many diseases are more of Anastasia's abilities. "Some kind of great power must have been concealed in the spiritual impulses of Anastasia, and this power seemingly overcomes darkness that has conquered the world," Vladimir Megre said in his excellent series of "The Ringing Cedars" books, which give many fabulous details about the life of Anastasia.

Anastasia said, "Fruits are designed to sustain Man's life more powerfully and effectively than any manufactured drugs of the present or future. These fruits are capable of counteracting and withstanding any disease of the human body. But to this end they must know about the human condition so that during the maturation process it can satiate its fruit with the right correlation of substances to heal a specific individual of his disease, if indeed he has it or is prone to it."

Anastasia added, "In order for the seed of a cucumber, tomato or any other plant grown in one's plot to have such information, the following steps are necessary. Before planting, put it into your mouth, under the tongue, for at least nine minutes. Then place the seen between the palms of your hands and hold it there for about thirty seconds. During this time it is important that you be standing barefoot on the spot of earth where you will later be planting it. open your hands and carefully raise the seed which you are holding to your mouth. Then blow on it lightly, warming it with your breath and the wee little seed will know everything that is within you."

Anastasia continued to explain: "Then you need to hold it with your hands another thirty seconds, presenting the seed to the celestial bodies. And the seed will determine the moment of its awakening. The plants will all help it. They will give the sprouts the light they need to produce fruit especially for you. After that you may plant the seed in the ground. In no case should you water it right off, so as not to wash away the saliva which is now covering it, along with other information about you that the seed will take in. It can be watered three days after planning. The planting must be done on days appropriate to each vegetable (people already know this, from the lunar calendar). In the absence of watering, a premature planting is not as harmful as an overdue planting."

Anastasia believes that these plants can cure all diseases in this manner using the plants' coding. This spiritual woman said, "Soften the dire in the excavated hold with one's fingers and toes. Any toxins are transmitted to the seeds. The fruit receives the diseases so that anyone who eats the fruit can overcome diseases. Sweet or sour cherries and flowers can be planted as well. It is an important thing to infuse the little patch of nature surrounding you with information about yourself. Only then will the healing effect and the life-giving support of your body be significantly higher."

Nonfiction

SIXTY-NINE

Phenomenal Discoveries at Lake Vostok

From 1947 to the late 1960s a number of books and magazine articles reported discoveries and evidence of large bodies of water and huge caverns beneath Antarctica. These subterranean zones were said to be inhabited by secretive colonies that fled the surface. It has become documented and verified that some 1940s German scientific expeditions were sent to try to explore and possibly colonize these regions of clean air and fresh water. Writers like Richard Shaver, Raymond Bernard, Michael Barton, Ray Palmer, Timothy Beckley and others produced books and magazine articles promoting their evidence of underground seas, lakes and inhabited caverns. A few expeditions claimed to have found tunnels near the north and south poles leading to these discoveries.

The most famous was Admiral Byrd and his "lost diary" which received extensive publicity in the first decade of the 2000s. Michael Barton and some other researchers wrote about Admiral Byrd's colleague Commander Bunger who discovered **unfrozen**, relatively **warm lakes** in Antarctica. In 1947 Commander Bunger reportedly landed his seaplane on lakes that had 65-70 degrees temperatures—instead of the expected 33 to 35 degrees (or more likely frozen) water in Antarctica's interior. The news account stated that Bunger's expedition found a small, forested, verdant, green oasis valley surrounded by ice stretching to the horizon on all sides! Huge ice cliffs surrounded this valley. It was speculated that these lakes were connected to hot geothermal geysers under the ice that led to water much deeper underground.

After appearing briefly in 1947 newspapers there was no further mention of this discovery. These claims of unfrozen Antarctic lakes remained a debatable mystery until January 2001. In *Scientific American* magazine there was a published account of a "gigantic" lake deep beneath the Antarctic ice sheet near the South Pole. This lake's dimensions are so huge that it sounds almost like science fiction. Lake Vostok is nearly a mile under the ice, yet is longer than two of the Great Lakes in the United States! This body of fresh, clean, clear water is reportedly an incredible 300 miles long! Forty-five states in America do not have lakes that big. The width is estimated approximately 50 miles which is wider than the distance most of America's islands are off coastlines.

There are few lakes in the USA as deep as this under-the-ice lake. An amazing discovery was the temperature of this lake beneath the ice. The warmest regions were an amazing 65 degrees! Much of the lake had water in the 50s instead of the expected low 30s in water surrounded by ice.

NASA and the Jet Propulsion Laboratory officially admitted the existence of Lake Vostok on January 24, 2001. An international expedition was being planned and formed to explore this lake. However, the civilians and foreign governments were mysteriously stopped by the National Security Agency (which is like the CIA in many ways) for "national security issues."

Why would this lake represent national security? Several researchers on Antarctica like Michael Barton, Al Bender, Linda Moulton Howe, Dr. Hank Krastman, Timothy Beckley and others published numerous accounts of the evidence of intense UFO activity over Antarctica. There are photographs of solid saucer-shaped and other types of UFOs taken by scientific expeditions in this polar region. UFOs were reportedly monitoring U.S. and foreign bases in Antarctica in the 1950s and 1960s.

One of the most documented and revealing accounts is Admiral Byrd's expedition that encountered flying disks coming from an opening in the ice sheet—detailed in the DVD "Admiral Byrd, the Hollow Earth Exploration and UFOs," by Dr. Hank Krastman (available from theUFOstore.com.) The late Admiral Byrd's once "secret diary" was downloaded off the Internet by Xian International's research team in 2007. Byrd allegedly discovered large inhabited caverns, lakes and was intimidated by under-ice based UFOs. Naturally, the Pentagon and U.S. military agencies would keep this discovery Top Secret like with many other UFO cases. It was not until after Admiral Byrd died that a relative obtained and released this diary. *Nexus* magazine from Australia did a great expose' of this Lake Vostok discovery and reading this back issue off the Internet for many details is highly recommended. A most recommended account of more details on this lake is William Eigles excellent article in *Atlantis Rising* magazine. This magazine has also done a great job covering alleged secret expeditions by Germans and others and claims of UFOs in this region. The lack of more news releases since 2001 indicates there is a big secret involving Lake Vostok. The official "environmental risks of invading a pristine environment" is an obvious poor reason to refuse the entry of environmental scientists from foreign universities and U.S. teams *not* affiliated with government/military/intelligence agencies. Officially and *legally* Antarctica is a "shared" continent by different nations and is used for scientific purposes and NOT military purposes. So, what is this "national security" all about? Antarctica is legally "international."

A large and strange magnetic "anomaly", at the north end of the lake was detected and photographed by NASA. Is this evidence of an under-ice secret base? The half mile high dome of air over the lake is surely enough room to construct a settlement.

A sidebar is that an even larger underground sea was found deep below China and announced in *Nexus* magazine. All of these back issues and their subterranean topics are listed in their magazine available in Borders and Barnes and Noble book stores (or contact them at: nexusmagazine.com.).

Some researchers also speculate about the possibilities of prehistoric life *still* existing in and surrounding Lake Vostok. The ice sheet has been covering this "sealed-off" ecosystem for tens of thousands of years and protecting it from the outside environmental damage.

Another source of this information was Debra Shingteller who mentioned the lake was near the Russian Vostok station about 300 miles from the South Pole. However, she refused to answer further inquiries. The late Russian scientist Ivan Takovoi discovered 200 square miles of "ice dunes" and thousands of "geothermal boils", up to hundreds of feet in diameter, in the ice sheet when stationed at the Russian research base. However, Ivan Takovoi disappeared in March 2000. An international team based at Cambridge University in London obtained NASA technology in February 2000 and planned to use robotic sensors and drill through the ice. There is no further information the mission.

On September 21, 1999, Roger Highfield was quoted in *The Electronic Telegraph*, "Lake Vostok especially fascinates scientists because it appears to have been isolated for millions of years, providing an opportunity for life to develop along a separate and perhaps different, evolutionary path. It is conjectured that microorganisms isolated for perhaps many millions of years from known terrestrial influences might be found in its sediments and waters, which could potentially yield promising new enzymes or antibiotics. Seminal insight into how ancient and contemporary microbes differ could develop as well, as a result. There is also scientific speculation that the ice bubbles and ice dome may contain so much methane that its release could endanger global climate and the chemistry of the atmosphere. Professor Thomas Gold of Cornell University believes in this methane theory and that drilling a hole to release it could be risky. The Russians at Vostok Station were planning to drill the ice.

Perhaps the huge amount of pure water in Lake Vostok could be tapped to provide all the thirsty and drought victims in the world with a water supply. Huge oil-tanker type ships up to a thousand feet long could transport this water to severe droughts. The water could be drilled and piped across Antarctica to be pumped on to waiting ships and fill their huge tanks. In foreign ports the water could be transported by tanker trucks and pipelines to supply people drinking polluted water or dying of thirst. It could be used to save their fruits and vegetables from droughts. Several other smaller lakes have also been discovered beneath the icecap in Antarctica. If people or ETs live under the ice in caverns they certainly have plenty of water.

There may be bacteria existing and expanding under the ice at Lake Vostok. Rumors have been circulated about a possible base developed by Germans who fled from Germany during World War II.

Nonfiction

SEVENTY

Magnificent Rainbows

The splendor of rainbows is magnificent. Hues of light reflect blue, green, pink, yellow and some orange in most rainbows. Rainbows appear suddenly to display rays of these beautiful colors in long lasting spectacular designs.

Rainbows are intriguing to many people. Songs, poems and stories have been written about rainbows. OVER THE RAINBOW sung by Judy Garland in the WIZARD OF OZ is a well known song about a rainbow.

We wonder what is at the end of a rainbow. Storytellers say there is a pot of gold at the end of a rainbow. When we stand at the end of a rainbow we see where the colors stop. Eventually rainbows disappear. They may reappear after it rains. They farm in a shape of a bow. They are called rainbows because mist from rain helps to create rainbows. Rainbows fascinate many people. They uplift us with their etheric appearance. People travel for miles to come close to rainbows. Their sudden appearance adds spectacular beauty in the sky. We are fortunate to witness the phenomenal existence of rainbows.

Rainbows appear around the whole Earth. Billions of people have witnessed magnificent rainbows. On Maui Island in Hawaii there are rainbows that are only one color. These bright, full rainbows are called "moonbows" because they are made by a full moon or a nearly full phase. These rainbows are only seen at night from specific angles and are extremely rare. The north coast of Maui is also the location of double and triple full rainbows. These are one to two rainbows in concentric half circles inside each other. The multiple full rainbows are also very rarely seen. An observer, Steve Omar lived on Maui about 40 years and only saw two moonbows and a few multi-rainbows. A few friends reported seeing these displays at different times and they are incredibly beautiful.